The Open University

A2 LATIN

Study Guide

This publication forms part of an Open University course A297 Reading Classical Latin. Details of this and other Open University courses can be obtained from the Course Reservations Centre, P.O. Box 724, The Open University, Milton Keynes MK7 6ZS, United Kingdom; tel. +44 (0)1908 653231, email ces-gen@open.ac.uk

Alternatively, you may visit the Open University website at http://www.open.ac.uk where you can learn more about the wide range of courses and packs offered at all levels by the Open University.

To purchase this publication or other components of Open University courses, contact Open University Worldwide Ltd, The Berrill Building, Walton Hall, Milton Keynes MK7 6AA, United Kingdom: tel. +44 (0)1908 858785; fax +44 (0)1908 858787; e-mail ouwenq@open.ac.uk; website http://www.ouw.co.uk

The Open University, Walton Hall, Milton Keynes MK7 6AA

Edited, designed and typeset by The Open University.

Printed and bound in the United Kingdom by The Alden Group, Oxford.

ISBN 0 7492 39689

2.3

28088B/a297sgi2.3

CONTENTS

The Production Course Team

Jonathan Davies	Graphic Designer
Robert Doubleday	Course Manager
Chris Emlyn-Jones	Reader
Robert Gibson	Compositor
Lorna Hardwick	Reader
Janet Huskinson	Reader
Paula James	Course Team Chair
Inga Mantle	Consultant
Sheila Page	Project Controller
Robert Philip	BBC Producer
Yvette Purdy	Course Manager
Wesley Semple	Reader
Jane Wood	Editor

The Presentation Course Team

Janet Huskinson	
Paula James	Course Team Chair
Dominic Montserrat	
Jane Wood	Editor
Roberta Wood	Course Manager

Acknowledgements

Special thanks are due to Dr Joan Booth of Swansea University. As External Assessor of A297, Dr Booth has read, commented in detail, and encouraged the Course Team writers at crucial stages. Her scholarship and specialist knowledge have been invaluable. Responsibility for any errors rests with the Course Team.

The Course Team would also like to acknowledge the Latin Committee of the Joint Association of Classical Teachers for allowing this Study Guide to draw on a draft of their *Independent Study Guide to Reading Latin. An Independent Study Guide to Reading Latin* by Peter V. Jones and Keith C. Sidwell was published by Cambridge University Press in November 2000.

The Committee of the Joint Association of Classical Teachers

Ken Dowden	The University of Birmingham
Lorna Kellett	Blyth Jex School, Norwich
Sally Knights	Filton College, Bristol
Alison Lewis	Teesside H.S., Stockton-on-Tees
Sarah Parnaby	Northwood College, Middlesex
Phillip Parr	The Haberdashers' Aske's School, Elstree
Helen Price	Westonbirt School, Tetbury
David Tristram	Weavers School, Wellingborough
Hilary Walters	Loughborough Grammar School

Cover illustration: 'Cave canem', mosaic. Museo Nazionale, Naples. Photograph: Alinari.

Introduction

written for the Course Team by Paula James

YOU ARE ASKED TO READ THIS INTRODUCTION BEFORE YOU START ON THE *READING LATIN* SET TEXTS.

Welcome to A297, Reading Classical Latin. This Study Guide is a key component of your course materials in the coming year. It contains detailed guidance on the best way to work through the course materials and pinpoints and explains challenging concepts. Don't neglect it!

The scope of the course

A297 is based on the Latin text books, *Reading Latin: Text* and *Reading Latin: Grammar, Vocabulary and Exercises*. For this course you are expected to study Sections 1–4 of the text books. By the end of the course you should have acquired a good understanding of Latin grammar, a considerable amount of vocabulary, and should be able to translate fairly long and complicated sentences in Latin. Latin is a rich and complex language with sophisticated forms. A number of these forms must remain beyond the scope of this course. You will have learned a considerable amount by the end of the course and should have a good grasp of working Latin but you should not expect to emerge from the course able to translate all original Latin texts.

By the end of the course you should have sufficient grounding in Latin to think about taking your study of Latin to a higher level. There is a whole section of the course books that is not covered by the course and this section leads you into continuous Latin of a more complex nature.

Finding your way around the course materials

Provided as part of your course materials, you have two volumes produced by Peter V. Jones and Keith C. Sidwell (published by Cambridge University Press) for people beginning to learn Latin at university level and/or as mature students. These are:

Reading Latin: Text (referred to as *RLT* in this Study Guide)

Reading Latin: Grammar, Vocabulary and Exercises (referred to as *GVE*).

You will be working through the first four sections of *RLT* and the associated *GVE* sections in this course.

This Study Guide contains commentaries to help you as you work your way through the course text books section by section, and, in Appendix 1, provides answers to the exercises that are set from *GVE*. Apart from this Study Guide, you also have a supplementary Translations Booklet and an audio-cassette tape, which, like this Study Guide, have both been prepared specially for Open University students.

The Translations Booklet provides you with an English translation of the passages that you will meet in *RLT*, but please take note from the outset that it is there for you to consult only *after* you have made valiant attempts to make sense of the passages yourself. The same is true of the answers to exercises in Appendix 1 at the back of this Study Guide.

The audio-cassette is divided into four bands. Band 1 contains a general introduction to Latin pronunciation, a short discussion on the way the Latin language works and a brief background of the genre of early Latin comedy. Band 2 introduces the playwright Plautus and discusses issues of performance. Band 3 introduces you to vital features of the language (with a little bit of humour thrown in!). It also provides a 'recital' of word endings in Latin, a tried and tested method of memorizing basic structures of the language. Band 4 is for the very end of the course and discusses the skill, structure and composition of Latin poetry.

The Study Calendar indicates when you should listen to each of the bands. Further information about the audio-cassette tape will be found in the booklet of Audio-cassette Notes.

Using the course materials

This Study Guide is designed to support you in your work with the Jones and Sidwell volumes in several ways. The Study Guide and Study Calendar will direct your work through *RLT*, section by section, along with the associated sections of *GVE*.

The usual pattern of study will be that you will translate the text in *RLT* as directed by the Study Guide, keeping to hand and working through the related section of *GVE*, where the grammar is explained and additional vocabulary is given. The exact order in which you tackle these elements will emerge according to your own preference. Since you will be working through a great deal of the text on your own, you may find it best to work through the grammar (and possibly also the exercises) *before* trying the translation of the running text as the course progresses. The explanatory grammar is likely to be a good place to begin each section as it will support you in grasping the sense of the running text as it becomes progressively more demanding.

When you tackle the translation passages in *RLT*, you may prefer to work out the sense of the passage in your head or to start out by writing your translation down. Use whichever method is best for you, unless you are specifically asked to write out a translation. The Translations Booklet provides translations of the *RLT* texts but you should take care to use this resource to check your work only *after* you have attempted the translation yourself, and not as a constant hand-holding facility when you are actually working through the passages. Please note that you *must* work through and make sense of *all* of the set translation passages in *RLT*.

GVE provides a great many practice exercises and **you will not have time to do them all**, so this Study Guide suggests which of the exercises are the most useful to work through for reinforcing and clarifying your understanding. You should consider these as set activities, representing the bare minimum of exercises that you must do in each section.

If you have time, you will also find the Reading Exercises very useful for consolidating your work in each section, but these are not considered as compulsory in this course. These exercises basically rehash the content and structures of the parallel running text in *RLT* and so provide useful further practice. You are advised to read the running text in *RLT* thoroughly and, if you are managing to go through the text twice, as suggested, then you may feel that the Reading Exercises in *GVE* are a dispensable luxury and may prefer not to spend extra time on them. However, they might prove very useful for exam revision.

The answers for all the set exercises are supplied in Appendix A at the end of this Study Guide, but again, please use these answers as a self-marking mechanism *after* you have completed the exercises. Additionally, the answers are also given for the optional Reading exercises and for selected other exercises that might be useful for revision.

This Study Guide provides a running commentary, in step with the course books, dealing with selected areas of the language work, and should be referred to alongside your study of both the *RLT* translation and the *GVE* exercises. The Study Guide commentary may not expand upon *all* the learning pressure points, but its additional explanations of certain aspects of the language should give you an extra perspective and a better understanding of the concepts.

Finally, you will, of course, need to memorize the grammar constructions and new vocabulary introduced in each section of the course, and regularly find time to revise grammar and vocabulary from your earlier study. The vocabulary that you should learn is listed section by section in the Assignment Booklet.

As you work through the course, you will soon get a 'feel' for the language and for the people whose identity and culture emerge through it. This process is what makes Latin such a rich and fascinating ancient language to learn.

Figure 1 Small fresco panel from House of Marcus Lucretius Fronto, Pompeii, showing a villa maritima. Photograph: Fototeca Unione, American Academy in Rome.

Pacing your work

The Study Calendar should never be far from your side. This timetable gives a detailed breakdown of the work you should aim to complete each week. For example, you are now in Study Week 1 of the course and the Study Calendar indicates that you should read this Introduction and listen to Bands 1 and 2 of the audio-cassette this week. In Study Weeks 2 and 3, you should work through Section 1A of *RLT* and attempt the recommended exercises in *GVE*. Two weeks have been allowed for Section 1A as you will be finding your way around some new terms and definitions, getting used to the structure of Latin sentences and so on.

You should move on to Section 1B in the fourth week of study, and should be ready to complete and submit the first assignment by the date marked on the Study Calendar. The week before the assignment is due has been left clear to allow you time to consolidate what you have covered so far, as well as to produce the assignment itself. You should continue at the steady pace laid out in the Study Calendar, and should have completed all the sections indicated before you tackle the second assignment.

With language study a particular kind of pacing is advisable. A phrase you will meet more than once is 'little and often'. This is not *one* possible approach to learning Latin; it is really the *only* way to succeed when you are studying an ancient language. You really need to set aside a realistic amount of time each week, and ideally a period each day, since progress is best made if learning is constantly reinforced. (Keep in mind that the expected study each week for a 30-point course is 7–8 hours.) The learning curve in language work is steady and progressive. You should be constantly building on previous stages. **It is not possible to miss out sections and recommended exercises in the hope of returning to them later. If you do this, you will lose your way in the language and the course.** Having said this, the Course Team is aware of and sympathetic to the fact that the reality of adult life is being beset with distractions and that other claims on your time can work against a regular rhythm of study. If for any reason you do fall behind, try to catch up in the next week, so that you are at the appropriate point in the work to cope with your next assignment.

The good news is that much of the preparatory and consolidation work you will need to do in order to progress can fit really well into busy lifestyles. The 'little and often' approach can be much more user-friendly than the prolonged and protracted learning session. For example, the vocabulary and grammatical sets for memorizing can be carried about on cards or in small exercise books and revised while you are on trains, tubes and buses, at spare moments through the day.

To sum up then, throughout this guide, I have suggested strategies for study, for ways of working and learning, and for retaining what you learn. The intention is not to be prescriptive especially in regard to your framework of study; you may have already developed very effective work patterns and ones that suit you and your particular circumstances as a distance learner. But the advice should help you to plan and pace your work.

Assessment strategy

Your four tutor-marked assignments (TMAs) will not be essays but a straightforward testing of your understanding of the language. The general pattern for each TMA is for Part 1 to require one-word answers identifying the correct Latin for an English phrase or word, and for Part 2 to consist of a piece of Latin prose for translation into idiomatic (natural-sounding) English. TMAs must be submitted to your tutor by the dates indicated in the TMA booklet (also shown on the Study Calendar) and will be marked and graded by your tutor. Your tutor's comments on your TMAs form part of the teaching strategy for the course and you should take note of the advice given in this feedback.

Tuition

One of the most enjoyable and enriching aspects of learning a language with the Open University is the experience of face-to-face tuition. If you are able to attend tutorials you will find them immensely valuable. However, do remember that whenever explanations need revisiting or teasing out, your tutor expects to hear from you and s/he is likely to give you convenient times to ring for a helpful discussion of any aspect of the course. Please contact your tutor as early in the course as possible and consult him or her about your study strategy.

As with other OU courses, your tutor will not only provide tutorial support, but will also grade and comment on your TMAs.

This Study Guide will act as an additional tutorial voice to support you through your work. You should return to the Study Guide at the beginning of each study section. Working through the *RLT* sections and consulting the Study Guide as you go, you should find that a fair few of your questions have been anticipated and that you have a friendly voice to listen to in moments of stress!

Further reading

There are a number of books about Roman history and civilization on the market. Any reading you can do in your spare time about Roman life will help to put the language you are learning into its historical and cultural context, for instance, the Penguin Plautus plays (in translation). The closer your acquaintance with the civilization of the Romans, the easier it will be to make sense of what they write about themselves and their society. However, no such further reading is prescribed or expected as an examinable part of this course.

Conventions used in this Study Guide

1 *RLT* = *Reading Latin: Text*

GVE = *Reading Latin: Grammar, Vocabulary and Exercises*

N.B. Page numbers come at the bottom of the page in *GVE*.

2 *V* and *U* are written in Latin with the same letter: capital *V*, lower case *u* – so we write *QVIS* in capitals but *quis* in lower case. (See p.xiv of *GVE*.)

3 Marking long vowels. You will notice that some vowels in *RLT* and *GVE* are marked with a macron (a bar above the letter), such as: ā ē ī ō ū. These markings indicate the pronunciation of so-called 'long vowels'. The pronunciations are given on p.xiv of *GVE*. The macra (plural of 'macron') not only help you pronounce the word correctly but can thus also help with meanings, since, as in English, words that are spelt the same but pronounced differently can have different meanings (for example, in English, the word 'lead'). You

do not need to put in the macron when you are writing Latin. So you can write *auarus* rather than *auārus*.

4 You will notice a marking: ‿ linking some words together. As explained on p.ix of *RLT*, these markings are provided as a translation aid and indicate groups of words that should be taken together; but again, you need not worry about including them in your own writing.

5 Literal translation. Sentences can be translated into English in various ways; the aim should be to keep to the original Latin phrasing without making the English sound too tortured and unnatural. English which keeps very close to the Latin but which does not really sound like familiar or idiomatic English is called a 'literal' translation. It is useful in so far as it demonstrates how the Latin language works. However, you should avoid forcing English into unnatural phrases when you do your own translations. You should aim to produce good natural-sounding English translations. With practice, you will soon become confident that the sense and meaning of the Latin are still being preserved.

ABBREVIATIONS

To simplify presentation this Study Guide uses the following abbreviations for common grammatical terms. (We will come on to their meanings in the next section.)

Abbreviation:	**Stands for:**
masc. *or* m.	masculine
fem. *or* f.	feminine
neut. *or* n.	neuter
sing. *or* s.	singular
pl.	plural
nom.	nominative
acc.	accusative
gen.	genitive
dat.	dative
abl.	ablative

The approach to Latin

written for the Course Team by Paula James and Chris Emlyn-Jones

Latin in the European context

The particular prominence of Latin in our everyday life can be explained by two significant historical developments. First is the importance of the language in the monastic tradition of European Christianity (and until quite recently, in the liturgy of the Roman Catholic church) and, along with Greek, in the terminology of intellectual traditions of philosophy, science and law in medieval, renaissance and (until the nineteenth century at least) modern culture. For example, 'essence' derives from the Latin *esse*, meaning 'to be'; similarly words such as 'substance', 'momentum', 'inertia', 'evidence', 'utilitarianism' and phrases such as *a priori* come directly from Latin.

The second development is easily demonstrated by the similarities between modern west European languages and can be traced back to the direct descent of these languages from Latin. We would expect the Roman influence to be pervasive in Italian but it is also prominent in French, Spanish, Portuguese, Romanian and other languages conventionally called 'Romance'. Of course, the Roman empire spanned the continent of Europe and beyond for hundreds of years, and language is not the only aspect of its wide cultural interaction.

The Romance languages have developed from dialect forms of Latin as it was spoken across the Roman empire and in areas where the Latin language was adopted as the main form of verbal and written communication. There are plenty of examples of words of this type; for instance, Latin *carus* (dear) has become *caro* in Italian, Spanish and Portuguese, and *cher* in French. The Latin *campus* (field) can be detected in the Italian, Spanish and Portuguese *campo* and in the French *champ*.

English belongs to the Romance languages (descended from Indo-European through Latin). For example, Latin *schola* (which in turn derives from the Greek word *schole*) has become English 'school', in company with Italian *scuola*, Spanish *escuela*, Portuguese *escola* and French *école*. However, Britain never developed Latin as a main spoken language in the way that France and Spain did. Rather, it developed a Germanic language, English, alongside the Celtic Welsh, Irish and Scots Gaelic. The resemblances between English and the Romance languages derive from a multitude of borrowings and adaptations from the period of the Roman occupation of Britain right up to the nineteenth century CE.

If Latin's place in the history of languages interests you, there is more detailed information in *GVE* pp.548–56 (Appendix: 'The Latin language').

What do we mean by 'grammar'?

Grammar is the system we use to facilitate our understanding of how a language works. Because it is a system it has certain organizing principles and a set of technical terms. At its most basic level the grammatical system helps us to see how a sentence is put together and how words relate to each other. Understanding the grammar of Latin is essential for an understanding of the meaning and spirit of the words on the page.

If you are innocent of grammatical concepts then you can start by making some exciting discoveries about your own language. If your mother tongue is one of the Romance languages, then you will have a head start on understanding how Latin works. If your first language has a different origin and history from the Indo-European family but you have become competent in English, then you have already acquired the enviable skill of learning a very differently structured language and Latin should hold no fears for you.

The next section of this Study Guide gives basic definitions and examples of grammar, first in relation to English and then to Latin. If you have never learned a language (modern, ancient or your own) in an analytical way, looking at structures and parts of speech, you should find the following introduction particularly useful. There is also a glossary of grammatical terms in *GVE* (pp.xvii–xxiii) which will be useful as a reference guide throughout your study.

Parts of speech and sentence structure

In order to understand and discuss grammar, you need to be familiar with the basic terminology. The explanations below give a slightly more expansive and helpful introduction to some essentials than the list of terms in the *GVE* glossary. You might not absorb all the information at once, but don't get anxious if this is the case. You will become familiar with the terminology as you begin to meet it and use it regularly.

A more detailed account of the functions of the parts of speech is given in the section on Latin Grammar on p.21 below, but the following notes are intended as a basic outline of how they work.

Every word can be classified as one of the following:

noun
pronoun
verb
adjective
adverb
preposition
conjunction
interjection.

These are known as the 'parts of speech' and each part of speech serves a particular function in a sentence. You will find them all (except interjection) defined in the *GVE* glossary. Briefly, their functions are as follows:

noun (*or* pronoun)	a name of a person, place, thing or abstraction, e.g. child, London, table, courage
verb	a word expressing action or state, e.g. run, jump, think, be
adjective	a word that describes ('qualifies') a noun or pronoun, e.g. red, clever, pretty
adverb	a word that describes ('modifies') a verb, e.g. quickly, enthusiastically
preposition	a word coming before a noun or pronoun to indicate the relationship of that word to other words, e.g into, from, by, over
conjunction	words that link parts of a sentence, e.g. when, and, but
interjection	an exclamation, e.g. Oh! Alas! Hurrah!

Nouns and verbs are the most important ingredients in sentences. The most straightforward type of sentence has somebody (noun) doing (verb) something.

Brutus	smiled.
NOUN	VERB

Nouns can also refer to abstract things:

Cleanliness	is	next	to	godliness.
NOUN	VERB	ADJECTIVE	PREPOSITION	NOUN

Pronouns stand in place of a noun. Words such as 'you', 'he', 'she', 'it', 'we' and 'they' are pronouns.

Adjectives are words that tell you something more about nouns: they are said to *qualify* the noun: 'This is a *steep* hill'; 'This hill is *steep*'. In both these cases, 'steep' is an adjective.

Adverbs tell us something more about how an action was performed: 'He spoke *impudently*'. Adverbs are said to *modify* a verb (a different term, notice, from the one used about adjectives, which *qualify* a noun or pronoun). Many adverbs in English end in '-ly', for example 'greedily', 'mostly'; but some do not, such as 'often', 'quite', 'much' (as in 'much more'), and 'fast' (as in 'How fast does your chariot go?').

Prepositions connect to a noun or a pronoun to indicate the relationship between words in a sentence. Words such as 'at', 'from', 'to', 'by', 'with' and 'of' are all prepositions. 'She's too good *for* him!' 'The cat sat *on* the mat.' In both Latin and English, prepositions in a sentence are said to govern nouns ('on *the mat*') and for this reason they have a special relationship with that noun. Prepositions can also govern pronouns.

Conjunctions provide links between phrases and sentences, for instance 'and', 'but', 'when', 'although', 'if'.

Interjections are stand-alone words as far as the structure of a sentence is concerned. They are exclamations that express emotion; for example, 'Alas!' and 'Hurrah!'.

Finally, there are two more important words to mention at this point. In English and many other languages, the words 'the' and 'a' (or 'an') are used to identify nouns. These are really a sort of adjective, but are called the *definite article* ('the') and the *indefinite article* ('a'). The important thing to remember about them in relation to Latin is that Latin doesn't have either of them.

In the following sentence, all the parts of speech are used. Try to identify them yourself before looking at the answer overleaf.

Well,	grammar	and	grammatical	terms

are	simple	for	us	when

we	see	them	in	action.

Figure 2 Pigeons, mosaic Museo Capitolini, Rome.
Photograph: Alinari-Anderson.

Well,	grammar	and	grammatical	terms
INTERJECTION	NOUN	CONJUNCTION	ADJECTIVE	NOUN

are	simple	for	us	when
VERB	ADJECTIVE	PREPOSITION	PRONOUN	CONJUNCTION

we	see	them	in	action.
PRONOUN	VERB	PRONOUN	PREPOSITION	NOUN

Starting with the sentence

Analysing a sentence is basic spade-work when you are learning Latin. Strictly speaking, a sentence should express a complete thought and contain a verb. A verb expresses an action or a state of being; for example, 'run', 'think', 'say', 'be' (this definition can be found in *GVE* p.xxiii). One word may serve as a sentence if that one word is a verb, for instance the command 'Go!', a short sharp order but a sentence, nevertheless.

Latin does not have to confine itself to the command form in order to produce a one-word sentence. We can translate the Latin word *timeo* as 'I am afraid'. Latin verbs contain within their endings the vital information of who is performing the action. *Timemus* is translated as 'We are afraid'. Note that the *-eo* of *timeo* has become the *-emus* of *timemus* but the root or stem *time-* indicates that we are still dealing with the same verb.

In English formal prose, punctuation divides sentence from sentence by capital letters at the beginning and full stops at the end. However, if you have ever written or read a leaflet, you will know that punctuation can be an unreliable guide in the search for a grammatically complete sentence.

'More wage cuts? Not on your life!' These are phrases not sentences because they do not contain a verb. However, they do express two thoughts quite clearly and could be interpreted as a political and economic statement or imply an ideological agenda. Nevertheless we have to be quite technical and formal about the sentence in order to get to grips with the structure of Latin.

Let us take a well-known English sentence and identify the two essential components, the subject and verb. *The cat sat on the mat* is a perfectly acceptable sentence. What we have here is *the cat*, centre stage, noun and subject. In the case of the cat, we could have used a pronoun and said *it sat on the mat* and we would still have had a legitimate sentence. *Sat* is a verb and indicates what the cat was doing. Remember that verbs express actions and conditions. Remember, too, that, in theory, you cannot express a complete sentence without a verb. *The cat* on its own would not have got us very far, but *the cat sat* tells a story, although it is a short one.

This is not the end of the sentence – we are given even more information about where the cat sat, i.e. *on the mat*. This may not give you a terribly thrilling or enlightening mental picture but it does introduce you to the joys of a prepositional phrase. The preposition in the prepositional phrase is the word *on*. Other examples of prepositions are words such as 'in', 'at', 'from', 'to', 'by' and 'with'. There are Latin words equivalent to many of the English prepositions: *in* for example, means the same in both Latin and English. In both languages prepositions in a sentence govern nouns (*on the mat* in our sample sentence) and for this reason they have a special relationship with that noun.

In Latin this relationship is clearly expressed not just by the indivisibility of the phrase – prepositions cannot generally be left hanging on their own without a noun or pronoun – but by changing the ending of the noun to reinforce its relationship with the preposition. In Latin, prepositions 'govern' the nouns they are linked to and can determine the ending of the noun, so that the noun itself signifies and reinforces its own role in the phrase.

This does not happen in English but in Latin the noun *mat* would need to be in a particular case, i.e. have a distinct ending associated with the preposition *on*. This is an example of the inflected nature of the Latin language and a good place to start in investigating the implications of inflection generally.

Latin grammar

An important feature of Latin is that it is an inflected language; that is, it changes the endings of nouns, pronouns, adjectives and verbs according to the context in which they are used. In traditional grammar, the system of inflection (the changing forms) of nouns, pronouns and adjectives is called *declension* (nouns and adjectives 'decline') and the system of inflection of verbs is called *conjugation* (verbs 'conjugate').

There are many patterns of word endings to learn, and it is a good idea to compile your own lists of them in a notebook, as you come across them.

Nouns

In English the relationship of words within a sentence is largely determined by position. In Latin, nouns have different endings depending on their role in a sentence. The different forms are called *cases* and each has a different word to describe it. The list of cases is as follows.

1 Nominative

The nominative is the case for the subject, i.e. for the person or thing doing something. '*Brutus* killed Caesar.' '*Rain* was falling'. In English, the subject almost always comes before the verb (although we sometimes meet an inverted construction such as 'said she' or 'alleged the President').

Watch out for nouns following the verb 'to be'. As a noun that follows the verb 'to be' refers to the same thing or person as the subject of the verb, giving us additional or alternative information about that subject, both nouns must be put in the nominative case. For example, 'Augustus is the emperor'. In this sentence it is quite clear that Augustus and the emperor are one and the same person. The grammatical term for this second noun, emperor, is the *complement* quite simply because it complements our information about Augustus and completes the sense of the verb. The complement denotes a noun following a verb but not in any way on the receiving end of an action. Think of it as the completing element, behaving in the same descriptive way as an adjective.

2 Vocative

This is the case for the names of people who are being addressed directly. '*Fido*, come here!' 'And now, *ladies* and *gentlemen*...'

3 Accusative

The accusative does more than one job.

(i) It expresses the direct object of a verb. The direct object is a noun or pronoun which in English usually follows the verb and is not introduced by a preposition. The direct object is on the receiving end of the action. 'Brutus killed *Caesar*.' Brutus is the subject, doing the killing. Caesar is the direct object, receiving the action of the fatal attack.

(ii) Prepositions meaning 'motion towards' and quite a number of others take the accusative – i.e. the noun they govern (are inseparable from) always goes into the accusative case (**to** the gate, *ad portam*).

It is interesting to think about this kind of case system in relation to modern English. Most words in English only really have a nominative and a genitive case:

	singular	**plural**
nominative	king	kings
genitive	king's	kings'

Even these few inflected forms in English are now falling into disuse and misuse, as fewer and fewer people know where to put the apostrophe ('). There are some accusatives left amongst the pronouns: 'him', 'her', 'me', 'them'; the obsolete 'thee' (nominative: 'thou'); and 'whom', which we do still encounter in modern English, as in the title of Ernest Hemingway's novel, *For Whom the Bell Tolls* (a line taken from the poet John Donne).

There is a popular tendency, which is often met with a wry smile from language scholars, to misuse or misapply the nominative form of the pronoun 'I' in English. Mistakenly thought to sound genteel, it is grammatically quite wrong to say 'between you and I' as the preposition 'between' requires the accusative 'me'. Similarly the sentence: 'He has made lunch for you and I'. What should it be?

4 Genitive
The genitive case denotes possession, equivalent to *-'s*, *-s'* or *of* in English (the king*'s*, kings*'*, *of* the king, *of* the kings).

5 Dative
The dative has various detailed uses; a very common one is the dative of the indirect object and in English accompanied by the prepositions 'to' and 'for'. 'I give a book *to him*'; 'I am providing this *for you*'.

Note the difference between the direct objects, 'book' and 'this', and the indirect objects, 'to him' and 'for you'. Although 'him' and 'you' are on the receiving end, they are not directly acted upon in the same way as the direct objects.

6 Ablative
Like the accusative, the ablative does more than one job.
(i) It expresses 'by' or 'with' a thing:
'He hit me *with* a club'; 'We will be coming *by* chariot'.
(ii) Prepositions amounting to 'from' and some others too, take the ablative: '*from* the gate'; '*out of* the town'.

There is also a locative case, which you will hear mentioned on the audio-cassette and will meet in *GVE* Section 4C. It will not figure largely in your life with Latin, however.

As in English, you can tell from the ending of a noun whether it is singular or plural ('king' or 'kings'). This is known as its *number.*

In Latin, nouns also have a *gender.* They belong to masculine, feminine or neuter groupings (*neuter* is the Latin for *neither* and indicates that the noun is *neither* masculine nor feminine but in a third category.) You would expect nouns such as 'father', 'mother', 'son' and 'daughter' to belong to masculine or feminine gender groups but in Latin you must also learn a gender designation for inanimate things and for abstract nouns.

Verbs

In English, in order to express a verb fully we need not only the verb itself but also information as to who is carrying out the action, i.e. a noun (or pronoun). This noun or pronoun (that is, the person who is carrying out the action) is called the 'subject' of the verb. In Latin, all this can be conveyed by a single word because the changeable ending of the verb carries information about the person performing the verb. Latin verbs thus have two elements:

1 a stem, the front part of the word, which does not generally change;
2 the ending, the end part of the word, which does change according to context.

For example, to say 'I love' in Latin we need just one word, *amo.* The *-o* ending indicates that 'I' am performing the action or having the feeling. If we wanted to say 'I would have loved', again Latin can express all this by changing the ending again: *amavissem. Amo* is still detectable but the new ending has altered the time of the action and also brought in room for doubt about the actual loving, a state English needed two more words to convey, i.e. 'would have'. Groups of words such as 'He-him-his', 'she-her-hers', 'I-me' and 'call-calls' demonstrate that English, too, sometimes changes forms of words depending on their function, but keep in mind that it does so much less frequently than Latin does.

Verbs in Latin have endings to indicate the following:

Voice

active:	Brutus *is killing* Caesar; it *is raining*.
passive (*GVE* p.243):	Caesar *is being killed* by Brutus.

Tense

present:	Brutus *is killing/kills* Caesar.
future:	Brutus *will kill* Caesar.
imperfect:	Brutus *was killing* Caesar.
perfect:	Brutus *killed/has killed* Caesar.
pluperfect:	Brutus *had killed* Caesar.
future perfect:	Brutus *will have killed* Caesar.

Mood

indicative:	Brutus *is killing/kills* Caesar.
subjunctive:	(survives in English – it's there in our 'would have loved' example on p.24, but is more pervasive and serves more functions in Latin. You don't meet the subjunctive mood until the fourth section of *RLT*)
imperative:	Brutus, *kill* Caesar.
infinitive:	*To kill* Caesar/*to have killed* Caesar. *To be going to kill* Caesar
participle:	*Killing* Caesar, he felt sick; *having killed* Caesar, he felt better.

Whatever the mood or the tense of the verb, verb endings will also show what person is performing the action.

person	singular	plural
1st	I	we
2nd	(thou), you	you
3rd	he, she, it	they

Another aspect of verbs is the *gerund*. An English example would be '*seeing* is *believing*' (although Latin would use the infinitive for this phrase, *uidere est credere* – 'to see is to believe'). In Latin there is also the *gerundive*, which has no real equivalent in English, but we have adopted some vocabulary words in English that are actually Latin gerundives, because they can be convenient and succinct; for example, the word 'agenda' is Latin for 'things that must be done'.

Adjectives

Adjectives in Latin have endings to match the specification of their nouns: they must be in the same case as their nouns and in the same number. But also, like nouns, they must show what gender the noun is – whether it is masculine, feminine, or neuter – and this can be a fairly arbitrary business in Latin.

Yes, men are masculine and women feminine, but the word for 'gate' (*porta*) is feminine, as are 'house' (*domus*) and mind (*mens*) and all sorts of words ending in *-tas*: *tempestas* (storm), *ciuitas* (state). *Ictus* (a blow) is masculine, *amor* (love) is masculine (but *cupido*, desire, is feminine!). *Bellum* (war) is neuter, as are *tempus* (time) and *cornu* (horn).

Participles and gerundives (see under Verbs, above) are treated as honorary adjectives and need to show case, number, gender.

Learning Latin words

Let us draw for a moment on the experience of encountering a foreign language. Picking up spoken language is obviously not an option with Latin, so the following discussion focuses on the written word. Translating from one language to another can be an exciting and stimulating activity. It involves a certain amount of interpretation and sometimes you have a choice of more than one equivalent for a particular word. In fact, translating is a cultural exchange which can enrich your understanding of your own language as well as of the one you are learning.

The bonus of translating from a heavily inflected language like Latin is the careful scrutiny each word demands in order to find out its exact function in relation to the words around it. It encourages you to be comprehensive in your approach, to take account of several different factors before you can be sure you have understood the word correctly.

The *meaning* of the Latin word *filius* is 'son' in English and that is how you will learn it in your word lists (vocabularies). In English the word 'filial' is recognizably from the Latin root. If you have not met the English word 'filial' before, look it up in a dictionary. Also related to *filius* are, not surprisingly, the Italian word for son, *figlio*, the French *fils*, the Romanian *fiu*, the Portuguese *filho* and, less obviously, at first sight, the Spanish *hijo*.

When you come across the Latin word *filia* you might assume a relationship with the Latin word *filius* and you would be right. *Filia*

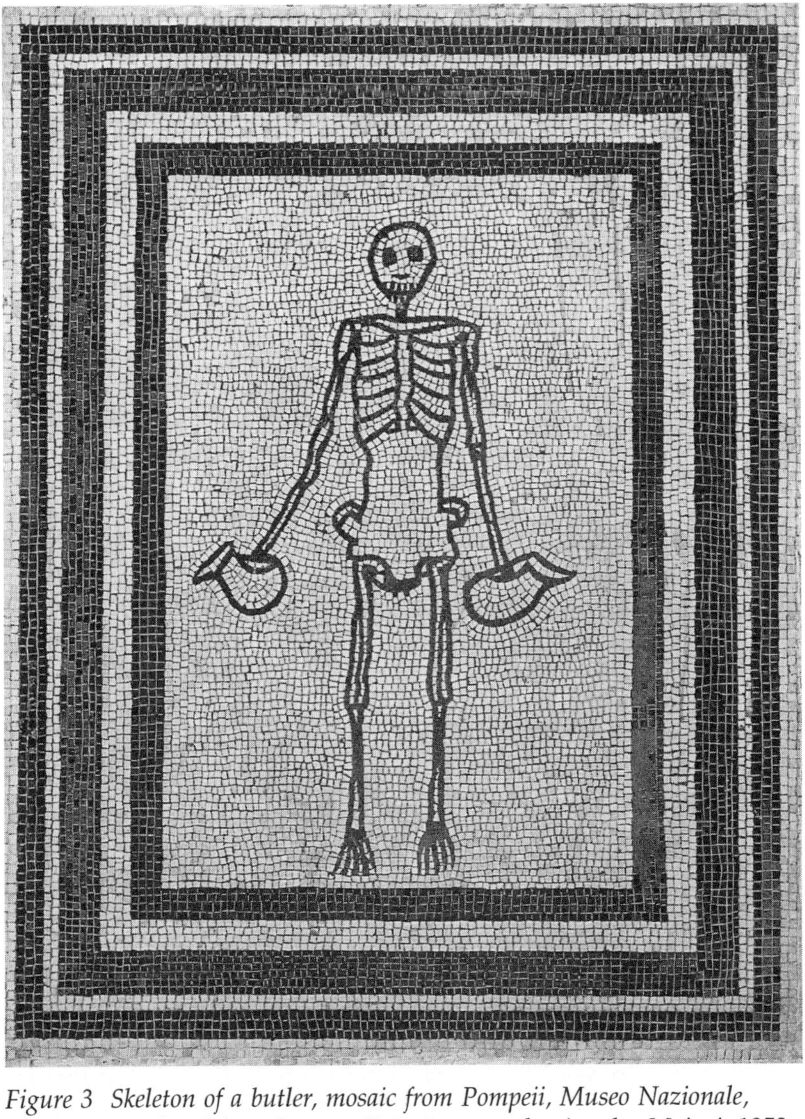

Figure 3 Skeleton of a butler, mosaic from Pompeii, Museo Nazionale, Naples. Reproduced from Roman Painting, *text by Amedeo Maiuri, 1953, Editions d'Art, Albert Skira, with permission of the publishers.*

means daughter and is a cognate of the word *filius*. In other words they look alike and come originally from the same word family. You will encounter a couple of cognates in your first section of text and grammar, *seruus* and *serua*, meaning male and female slave. (English 'servile' and 'servant' – the first *u* in the Latin words is pronounced as a *w* sound but it corresponds to our letter *v*. There is an explanation of this in Band 1 of the audio-cassette.)

By looking closely at these examples we have found out about Latin cognate or related words. You have now encountered several examples of European derivatives of Latin words. You might have noticed another distinguishing feature of the examples we just discussed, that the words denoting males ended in *-us* and those denoting females ended in *-a*; well done, if you did get this last point. All these things give clues to a word's function and meaning. There will be times when apparent similarities are misleading, so-called 'false friends', but there will be plenty of occasions when you can work out a Latin word internally, by reference to another Latin word, or by recognizing it from an English or European derivative.

Section One

1 Read the brief introduction to Plautus on *RLT* p.1.

2 Listen to Audio-cassette Band 2.

3 Read on in this Study Guide for help with approaching Section One of *RLT*.

Section 1: Plautus' *Aulularia*
Section 1A

Section 1 of *RLT* is based on a play by Plautus, *Aulularia* ('The pot of gold').

As you come to translate the Latin, you may stumble occasionally over meaning. Remember that the verb is the anchor of the sentence so make sure you have identified it as soon as possible.

It's probably best not to dwell on a sentence or phrase you find difficult but to return to it after you have read through the notes and done the exercises in *GVE*. If that does not clarify the awkward passage, then, *and only then*, check out the translation provided in the Translations Booklet. Make sure that you understand how the English version has been arrived at.

There is plenty of guidance in *GVE* for this first section. You may find the detailed dissection of sentences and structures *GVE* provides almost too much information but actually this attention to detail is very important for your study. Also the painstaking approach should clarify areas already raised in this Study Guide and in *GVE*'s own introduction and grammar glossary.

You are now ready to make sense of the Latin on *RLT* pp.2–6. Do not try to do too much at once! The golden rule bears repeating; remember, when learning any language it is best to work on the principle of 'little and often' (especially 'often'). Keeping this Study Guide and the relevant part of *GVE* to hand (pp.1–4 initally), work through the text in *RLT*, referring to the commentary below as you go along, as appropriate.

RLT pp.2–3 Introduction

RLT p.2 introduces the cast list. The purpose of the text on this page is to familiarize you with the verb 'to be', *esse* in Latin.

GVE tells you that in Latin there is no need to attach a separate word for the subject personal pronoun. In Latin *sum* is the equivalent of two English words, *I am*. *Es* means *you are* and so on. However, the cast list does add in Latin personal pronouns, *ego*, *tu*. When they do appear they are extras for emphasis. Each character needs distinguishing; for instance: *ego sum Euclio* – *I* am Euclio.

Note carefully what *GVE* says about word order: subject, complement and verb. The complement is defined for you on p.xviii of *GVE* and is discussed further in the introduction to this Study Guide. With the verb 'to be', *esse*, and also with verbs such as *seem*, and *appear*, we can be given two pieces of information about a character's identity. So we find out in the sentence *Euclio senex est* that Euclio is an old man. Old man *complements* or completes the information we have already about his name. I am driving this point home because the complement must not be confused with the object of a verb! Euclio and the old man are the same person.

Once the characters of the play have been described, they go into action (Scene I). You have moved from the verb conveying a condition to the verb as an action word. Most of the verbs you meet in Section 1A belong to the first conjugation (the family of verbs with an 'a' stem). A few have an 'e' stem and these are second conjugation verbs.

The only verbs not conforming to the above patterns are *aperit*, a stage direction, line 24, p.4 and *cognoui*, line 36, p.5. They are both translated in the vocabulary list and you will meet their conjugation patterns in due course.

By the way, you may have noticed a bit of a mix-and-match in the stage directions. Occasionally they appear in English but most of them are in Latin and you should have a go at translating the Latin into English.

You are confined to the present tense of the verb in 1A. It suits the dramatic medium very well and lets you into verb forms gently. Make sure that you do translate the present tense in Latin by the present tense in English. It can be easy to slip into past or future tenses if you are not vigilant. *GVE* prints the first and second conjugations, present tense on pp.4–5.

Exercises

Attempt the following exercises from *GVE*.

p.4 Morphology: 1–2
p.4 Reading: (a)–(h)
p.4 English–Latin: (a)–(f)

Vocabulary

Learn Learning vocabulary for Introduction (Assignment Booklet).

RLT pp.3–6

Translate the text, using the vocabulary (*GVE* pp.5–7) and grammar notes (*GVE* pp.7–13) to help you.

Additional grammar notes

The *Reading exercise*, 3(a) and (b), on p.16 of *GVE*, encourages you to identify subject, object and prepositional phrasing. If you would prefer to cut your teeth on some structurally simpler English poetry, try identifying parts of speech (nouns, adjectives, verbs and so on, as well as subjects and objects), in the nonsense poem extract below. For instance, in the first line we could speculate that 'toves' might be some kind of creature and therefore they would come into the category of nouns. 'Slithy' can then be identified as an adjective describing the 'toves', and so on.

Jabberwocky

'Twas brillig and the slithy toves
Did gyre and gimble in the wabe;
All mimsy were the borogroves
And the mome raths outgabe.

"Beware the Jabberwock, my son!
The jaws that bite, the claws that catch
Beware the Jubjub bird, and shun
The frumious Bandersnatch!"

He took his vorpal sword in hand.
Long time the manxome foe he sought –
Then rested he by the Tumtum tree
And stood awhile in thought.

Lewis Carroll

Exercises

Attempt the following exercises from *GVE.*

p.9	Exercises 1–3
p.13	Exercises: 1–3 (N.B. all nouns are either nominative or accusative)
p.14	Exercise: Write the Latin for... (in the middle of the page)
pp.16–17	Reading exercise: 4
p.17	English–Latin (N.B. Don't be tempted to translate the 'it is' in brackets. This is simply the English way of emphasizing what the slaves are carrying. Latin achieves the same effect with the word order.)

If you have time, also attempt:

pp.15–16	Reading exercise: 1, 3(a) and 3(b) (see also the activity suggested below)

Vocabulary

Learn the vocabulary for 1A as listed in the Assignment Booklet.

The verbs *uoco* and *clamo*, which both appear in the Learning Vocabulary at this point, both have a meaning connected to 'calling', but you will see from the context in the *RLT* passage that *uoco* implies summoning someone whereas *clamo* is a general shout or ex*clama*tion. The verb *uoco* can take a direct object and for this reason is what we call a 'transitive' verb, e.g. *Euclio seruum uocat* – 'Euclio summons the slave' whereas *clamo* in this passage is intransitive and does not take a direct object: *Euclio clamat* – 'Euclio calls out'.

Finally, for Section 1A...

- Ensure that you know all the grammar for the Introduction and Section 1A, especially the endings of the nouns and verbs. Recite them in their due order until you have memorized them.
- Read again *RLT* pp.2–3.

Section 1B

RLT pp.6–8

Translate the text, using the vocabulary (*GVE* pp.18–19) and Grammar notes (*GVE* pp.20–25) to help you.

Additional grammar notes

Amare and *habere* are infinitives, the part of the verb we express by putting 'to' in front; for example, 'to love', 'to have'. (In other European languages such as French, German, Italian and Spanish, the infinitive of a verb is just one word, as in Latin; for instance, the French *aimer,* meaning 'to love' and the Spanish *tener,* 'to have'.)

The infinitive has no direct attachment to any person but it is enormously useful to know the infinitive form of verbs in Latin for this can give a firm clue about their conjugation patterns (whether they are 'a' stem, 'e' stem or 'i' stem verbs, for instance). *GVE* does not introduce you to the nature and function of the Latin infinitive until Section 1F but you will find it helpful to find out the infinitive of each verb as you meet it from this point on.

Exercises

Attempt the following exercises from *GVE.*

p.22	Exercises: 1–3*
p.24	Exercises: 1–3
pp.25–6	Exercises: 1–5**
p.29	Reading exercise/Test exercise

If you have time for further practice, also attempt:

p.28	Reading exercises: 2–3

* Exercise 3 does not continue to emphasize the direct objects even when they appear first in the sentence.

** *GVE* p.26 question 2 is on agreement of adjectives. Note that agreement of adjectives does not mean that the endings of nouns and adjectives will necessarily always look the same or be matched in sound, for example, *multi fures* – many thieves (nominative masculine plural).

Vocabulary

Learn the vocabulary for 1B as listed in the Assignment Booklet.

When learning nouns and verbs it is helpful to keep lists, putting them in columns according to their declension or conjugation; for nouns, for example:

First declension	*Second declension*	*Third declension*
cura, curae fem. *corona, coronae* fem.	*deus, dei* masc. *coquus, coqui* masc. *aurum, auri* neut.	*fur, furis* masc. *senex, senis* masc.

and similarly for verbs:

First conjugation	*Second conjugation*
amare	*habere*

Add the other conjugations as they occur.

Finally, for Section 1B...

- Ensure that you know all the grammar for Section 1B, especially the endings of third declension nouns. Although *aedes* is used in its plural form for 'house' in the Reading Text, it is rather a bothersome noun to use as a model because of its eccentricity. In its singular form it means 'temple' or 'room'. *Ignis,* which you will meet in Section 1C, is a better model to follow for 'i' stem third declension nouns.
- Ensure that you know all of the vocabulary so far.
- Read again *RLT* pp.6–8.

Section 1C

RLT pp.8–10

Translate the text, using the Vocabulary (*GVE* pp.35–6) and Grammar notes (*GVE* pp.37–40) to help you.

Additional grammar notes

In case you had any difficulties with the explanation on p.39, note 3 (the objective genitives), here is further clarification.

If you were putting 'My love is like a red, red rose' into Latin, you would start with *amor meus* because the love is a feeling which belongs to you. You need *meus,* which behaves like an adjective but also demonstrates possession and is related to the pronoun, *me.*

If you were translating the sentence, 'Love of/for me is quite understandable', you would start with *amor mei* (using the genitive case of the personal pronoun). It might help to split the sentence into 'They (person or persons unknown) love me. This is quite understandable.' This is where the *object* element of the *objective genitive* manifests itself, in that *me* is clearly the direct object of 'love' when the sentiment is expressed using a verb.

Exercises

Attempt the following exercises from *GVE.*

p.37	Exercises: 1–3
p.38	Exercises: 1–2
p.39	Exercises: 1 (*meus* only) and 2
p.40	Exercises: 1–3
p.41	Exercise: top of page
pp.42	Reading exercise/Test exercise
pp.42–3	English–Latin

Vocabulary

Learn the vocabulary for 1C as listed in the Assignment Booklet.

Finally, for Section 1C...

- Ensure that you know all of the grammar for Section 1C.
- Ensure that you know all of the vocabulary so far.
- Read again Section 1C, *RLT* pp.8–10.

Section 1D

RLT pp.10–12

Translate the text, using the vocabulary (*GVE* pp.45–6) and grammar notes (*GVE* pp.47–51) to help you.

Additional grammar notes

Quis? Qui? When you are learning the interrogative pronouns and adjectives, *quis? qui?*, it would be a good idea to write them out afresh, separating out the interrogative and the adjectival *quis, qui*. Their doubled-up layout on p.50 of *GVE* is not a happy saving of space.

Third declension nouns. Remember that it is only in the nominative or vocative singular that third declension nouns (and the same goes for the third declension adjectives) seem to be so varied in form. Once past the nominative and vocative, they basically behave in the same way.

Exercises

p.48	Exercises: 1–3
p.50	Exercises: 1 (*miser* and *pulcher* only) and 2
p.51	Exercises 1
pp.54–5	English–Latin

If you have time, also attempt:

pp.52–3	Exercises: 1–6
p.53	Reading
p.54	Reading exercise/Test exercise

Vocabulary

Learn the vocabulary for 1D as listed in the Assignment Booklet.

Finally, for Section 1D...

- Ensure that you know all of the grammar for Section 1D, especially the noun and verb endings.
- Ensure that you know all of the vocabulary so far.
- Read again *RLT* pp.10–12.

Section 1E

RLT pp.12–14

Translate the text, using the vocabulary (*GVE* p.57) and grammar notes (*GVE* pp.58–61) to help you.

Additional grammar notes

Questions with *-ne*. Remember this is an economical way to express a question and should not be confused with negative *ne* when you encounter it.

Exercises

p.60	Exercises: 1–2
p.61	Exercises: 1
pp.61–2	Exercises: (a)–(j)
p.62	Exercises 1–3
p.63	Reading exercises: 1
p.64	Reading exercise/Test exercise
p.64	English–Latin

If you have time, also attempt:

p.61 Exercises: 2

In this exercise, decide first the case, gender and number of the given form of *pulcher*; check alternatives (see *GVE* pp.48–9). Also check carefully the declension and gender of each noun before deciding what case it is.

Vocabulary

Learn the vocabulary for 1E as listed in the Assignment Booklet.

Finally, for Section 1E...

- Ensure that you know all of the Grammar for Section 1E, especially the forms of *uolo* and *fero* and the endings of all imperatives.
- Ensure that you know all of the vocabulary so far.
- Read again *RLT* pp.12–14.

Section 1F

RLT pp.14–17

Translation

Translate the text, using the vocabulary (*GVE* p.67) and grammar notes (*GVE* pp.68–72) to help you.

Additional grammar notes

In general, third declension adjectives have the same endings as third declension nouns – except that the ablative singular usually ends in *-i* and not *-e*. Learn these adjectives in the following pattern and you should have few problems in dealing with them.

First and second declension adjectives

bon*us*	bon*a*	bon*um*	=	good
mis*er*	miser*a*	miser*um*	=	wretched
pulch*er*	pulchr*a*	pulchr*um*	=	beautiful

Third declension adjectives

ing*ens*	ing*entis*	=	huge
auda*x*	auda*cis*	=	bold
omn*is*	omn*is* (but note that *omnis* in the nominative goes *omnis, omnis, omne*)	=	all

Notable features of third declension adjectives

For all those adjectives which have only one form in the nominative (*audax, ingens* etc.) you need to learn the genitive singular because this is the only way you can see the stem (*audacis, ingentis*). You also need to learn the top horizontal line of nominative singulars for third declension adjectives which have two forms in the nominative, one for the masculine and feminine and another for the neuter (e.g. *omnis, omnis, omne*), because that is the key to their stem.

Additional grammar notes

Like the third declension nouns, third declension adjectives are not as variable and capricious in their patterns as they might appear at first sight. You have seen how those on the pattern of *omnis* reveal their stem in the nominative form and so their inflection pattern can be worked out from then on. Adjectives such as *ingens* and *audax* do not reveal their stem in the nominative form. We need to find out their genitive singular (as we do with nouns) in order to know how they decline. The same formula applies with slight variations with adjectives such as *diues*, *uetus* and *pauper.*

Exercises

p.69	Exercise: centre of page
pp.71–2	Exercises: 1–3
p.73	Exercises: 1–3*
pp.74–5	Reading exercise/Test exercise

If you have time, also attempt:

p.75 *English–Latin*

* N.B. Adjectives can be used on their own without a noun (see *GVE* p.23, note 7)

Vocabulary

Learn the vocabulary for 1F as listed in the Assignment Booklet.

Finally for Section 1F...

- Ensure that you know all the grammar for Section 1F, especially infinitives and third declension adjectives.
- Ensure that you know all of the vocabulary so far.
- Read again *RLT* pp.14–17.

Section 1G

RLT pp.17–20

Translate the text, using the vocabulary (*GVE* pp.77–8) and grammar notes (*GVE* pp.78–80) to help you.

Exercises

pp.79–80	Exercises: 2–4
pp.80–81	Exercises: 2–5
pp.81–2	Reading Exercises: 1–2
p.83	English–Latin

If you have time, also attempt:

p.82	Reading exercise/Test exercise

Vocabulary

Learn the vocabulary for 1G, as listed in the Assignment Booklet.

Finally for Section 1G...

- Ensure that you know all the grammar for Section 1G, especially the various uses of the dative.
- Ensure that you know all the vocabulary so far.
- Read again *RLT* pp.17–20.

You have now finished Section One of *RLT* and should have acquired a basic understanding of how the language works. If you feel uncertain of any points, go over the relevant sections again. You will probably find that what you found difficult at the first attempt is now much easier.

If you have not already done so, go through the *Deliciae Latinae* which come at the end of each sub-section. These pages will not only help you with your vocabulary but will also enable you to appreciate the Latin language in its cultural setting and to see how modern languages have developed from Latin.

This is a good place to listen to the recital of paradigms (audio-cassette Band 3) which covers nouns, pronouns, adjectives and verbs you have learned so far. Ignore paradigms you have not met, for the present.

Section Two

The Study Guide commentary on Section One gave clear instructions on how to use and work through *GVE*. From this point on, the Study Guide will be more discursive, discussing points of interest and clarifying new concepts as they appear. The learning agenda in 2A is a varied one, which makes it interesting but demanding. Don't rush at this section – the Study Calendar allows two weeks' study for it.

It would be a tall order to work through all the exercises, so focus on the ones set in each section. You may wish to come back to some of the other exercises for exam revision, or use them towards the end of the course for further practice if you identify a weak area in your understanding.

For Sections Two–Four, follow the same pattern of study as you did for Section One. Take each part of a section at a time, go through the text and work out the meaning with the help of the notes in *GVE*. Learn the vocabulary as given in the section-by-section lists in the Assignment Booklet, and do the set exercises, checking the answers as you go. Appendix 1 in this Study Guide provides answers for all of the set exercises and also for the optional Reading exercises and some selected others which may be useful for further practice. You are advised also to go through the *Deliciae Latinae* for each section; this will help you with vocabulary, as well as putting the language and culture into context.

Section 2A

p.88 The future indicative active

In Section 2A you meet the future tense, and the more you practise this tense, the better. By the way, verbs that end in *-bo* in the present tense, such as *scribo*, 'I write', may fool you momentarily if the future tense is a recent acquaintance. You should be able to work out for yourself why this is so.

pp.89–90 Irregular verbs

The irregular verbs, accessibly set out on *GVE* pp.89–90, will become familiar in time. Return to *GVE* p.59 at this point and revise *uolo* before plunging in here, and then set out all four verbs together in your personal notebook on verbs. There are not many abnormally behaving verbs in Latin and their very distinctiveness can be an aid to memorizing them. Exercises 1 and 2 (p.90) are a useful test of *possum, nolo, malo*.

p.91 Adjectives

The key to success when learning adjectives, as *GVE* occasionally reminds you, is to be fully aware of the declension you are dealing with. Just as you need to find out the grammatical status of a noun in order to sort out its pattern of inflection, so you also need to know where the adjectives belong. For instance, the noun *puer* ('boy') is a second declension noun whereas *pater* ('father') follows the third declension pattern. On the same principle, the adjective *celer* ('speedy') is third declension and so cannot be declined on the second declension pattern of the adjective *miser* ('wretched').

Remember that even a pocket Latin dictionary will give both the nominative and the genitive singular of the noun and, where necessary, of the related adjective, and this second piece of information will indicate the appropriate declension.

p.93 Fourth declension nouns

The advice above about double-checking declensions needs to be universally applied to your learning experience. The model noun *manus* ('hand') is neither second declension masculine like *seruus* nor third declension neuter like *tempus*. Instead it seems to exist in a paradigm of its own. Actually, if you look closely (and of course you are going to learn it off by heart!) you'll see that it is not so individual or free-standing but combines second and third declension endings. This realization might demystify the pattern.

You may find the Latin sentence below an interesting one: it demonstrates the challenge of the inflected language for those of us who are simply not used to such a rich weave of word endings. It perhaps points up, too, the hurdles we face if we try to 'translate as we go' without the benefit of the Roman mindset. *GVE* is perfectly right to suggest that this is the least artificial and contorted way to deal with a Latin sentence but in the early days the 'dissect and re-order' approach may be the most practical method of arriving at a translation which makes sense.

militi dant dona puellae.

The word order of this sentence combined with cursory reference to the dictionary or instant recall of the vocabulary might lead you to translate this sentence as: 'The soldiers give gifts to the girl'. Unfortunately, this will not work. If you remind yourself that the word for 'soldier', *miles*, is a third declension noun, then you will speedily see that *militi* can only be dative singular not nominative plural (although an '*-i*' ending is a nominative or subject ending for second declension nouns). What would the nominative plural of *miles* be? (Answer in footnote below[1].)

You must look elsewhere for the subject of the verb *dant* which is a third person plural ending in the present tense. *Dona* (gifts) could be the subject as this form could be a neuter plural nominative (*donum* is a second declension neuter noun) but then neither *militi*, as discussed, nor *puellae* will do as the direct object (the thing being given). Sense should tell you that the gifts are the things being given, but if we want to exclude the word *puellae* (girls) on grammatical grounds, then the direct object or accusative form would have to be *puellas*, not *puellae* (*puella* is a first declension feminine noun).

There is only one way this sentence can make sense grammatically and that is the following translation:

> The girls [nominative plural] give gifts [accusative plural] to the soldier [dative singular].

It was no use relying on the word order for sense here, as for some reason 'soldier' (*militi*) had a privileged first position. (This word

[1] Answer: *milites*

order could suggest a translation with an emphasis on the soldier: 'It is the soldier the girls give gifts to'.)

This analysis of the syntax, the way the sentence is structured, demonstrates how vital it is to know how different declensions behave, especially when word order can be flexible, in the interests of emphasis, or where poetry is concerned, to maximize variety of sound and metre.

Endnote

GVE is a little cavalier with its statements on p.93. *Manus* with a short '*u*' can only be nominative singular, this is true; but if you come across it in any future prose text which does not mark long vowels with macra, you'll be spoilt for choice as far as identifying the case is concerned. Only context will reveal whether unmarked *manus* is nominative singular, nominative plural, accusative plural or genitive singular.

Just a few words on gender – look out for the misprint on p.153 of *GVE*, where *manus* is wrongly labelled as masculine. Also, saying that most fourth declension nouns are masculine may be misleading. The Latin words for different species of trees are usually feminine and some of these words have fourth declension '*-us*' endings (e.g. *quercus, quercus,* the oak tree, a noun which, like *domus,* sports both second and fourth declension endings). Some trees are second declension feminine nouns (e.g. *ulmus,* the elm tree).

Exercises

p.89	Exercises: 1–5
p.90	Exercises: 1–2
p.93	Exercises: 1–2
p.94	Exercises: 1–2
pp.96–7	Reading exercise/Test exercise
p.97	English–Latin

Vocabulary

Don't forget to make sure that you know all the vocabulary to date.

Section 2B

pp.102–4 Deponent verbs

The deponent endings introduce you to the look and shape of the passive voice. Any active verb which takes a direct object (the technical term is *transitive* verb) can have a passive voice. For instance, 'I call' can be turned into 'I am called'; *uoco* becomes *uocor.* You may remember the distinction made between *uoco* and *clamo* on p.32. *Clamo* cannot be used in quite the same way but *clamo* could take a direct object of a person (call upon) or of a thing, e.g. *magnum clamorem clamo!* ('I shout out a loud shout!')

You will meet the passive voice and a more thorough explanation about its uses and meaning at a later stage, but it is good to be aware of what's on the horizon, especially when it sets this new form in a broader context. The deponent verb has an active sense but a passive appearance, and meeting it here acquaints you with endings that you will need to know when you meet the passive of active verbs. Cherish the deponents, because learning their forms now will save you time in the future.

pp.105–6 Fifth declension nouns, third declension nouns and special adjectives

The fifth and third declensions and two irregular adjectives complete your learning tasks in 2B. As usual there is no effective substitute for rote learning (and don't forget that reciting the declensions out loud and listening again to the examples on Band 3 of the audio-cassette are recommended reinforcements).

p.107 Reading exercise

Do note that Latin is a more rigorous time-keeper than English when it comes to the tense of the verb. The word 'tense' derives from the Latin for 'time', *tempus,* and a vital function of the verb is telling the time: when, exactly, is the action taking place? The precision timing of Latin comes to the fore in the Reading exercise on p.107, sentences (a)–(c), where a more natural-sounding English translation will not use the future tense as often as Latin does (even when the action is clearly taking place in the future). This is one of the very few occasions when you are allowed – indeed encouraged – to translate a Latin tense by a different, not a corresponding, tense in English.

Exercises

p.104	Exercises: 1–4
p.105	Exercise (*Translate...*); Exercise (*Decline...*)
pp.106–7	Exercises: 1–2
p.107	Reading: (a)–(e)
p.108	Reading exercise/Test exercise

Vocabulary

Ensure that you know all the vocabulary to date.

Figure 4 Italian marble relief of coppersmith's workshop, probably a shop sign, from Pompeii Museo Nazionale, Naples. Photograph: Alinari.

Section 2C

pp.113–4 *Hic haec hoc*

You continue your discovery of pronouns with *hic haec hoc*. This is featured on the audio-cassette readings so listen to the relevant section of Band 3 as part of your study of this section. *Hic haec hoc* should, in all its forms, become second nature to you, along with *ille illa illud* (and eventually *is ea id*, which you will meet in Section 3A).

Exercises

p.115	Exercises: 2, 3, 4, 5
p.115	Optional revision: 1, 2
p.116	Exercises: 1, 2, 3
p.117	Reading exercise/Test exercise
pp.117–8	English–Latin

Vocabulary

Ensure that you know all the vocabulary to date.

Figure 5 Still life with eggs and game, from the house of Julia Felix, Pompeii Museo Nazionale, Naples. Reproduced from Roman Painting, *text by Amedeo Maiuri, 1953 Editions d'Art, Albert Skira, with permission of the publishers.*

Section 2D

pp.122–4 The perfect tense (completed actions in the past)

Here you meet another set of endings attached to this new tense but with the familiar faces of the model verbs. The perfect endings are not too difficult to learn but the preceding stem of each verb can and often does change. Don't be discouraged by verb stems that take unexpected turns. Take heart from the fact that there are plenty of challenges in English past tenses too, which the learner of English has to accept and get used to. These might involve a simple vowel change or even an unrecognizable transformation in either or both the perfect tense and the past participle. For instance, *do did done; go went gone; see saw seen; drink drank drunk; lie lay lain.*

There is a helpful summary of irregular verbs so far on pp.124–6. Do get into the good habit of learning the principal parts of each new verb. These four parts will be an invaluable guide to the verb in all its manifestations (and dictionaries will either indicate that the verb straightforwardly follows a conjugation pattern or they will provide you with its particular variations by means of the principal parts). Exercise 3 on p.126 provides good practice in recognition.

pp.126–7 The ablative

This is the section in which you are alerted to a further use of the ablative. It's never too soon to start making your own table of uses for all the cases.

Exercises

p.126	Exercises: 1–5
p.127	Exercise: 1
p.128	Reading exercise/Test exercise
pp.128–9	English–Latin

Vocabulary

Ensure that you know all the vocabulary to date. Please note that in the Learning vocabulary on p.121 of *GVE*, *forum* is given the incorrect gender. It should be labelled as neuter, not masculine.

Section 2E

pp.134–5 Future deponent

Here you have the future of the deponent verb. *GVE* alerts you to an alternative to the second person singular. As this *-ere* ending occurs quite regularly in literary Latin, it has been introduced at this early stage. As long as you can recognize it, in other respects it can be safely stored in the back of your mind at this early stage.

Exercises

pp.135–6	Exercises: 2, 3, 6
p.136	Exercises: 1
pp.137–8	Reading and reading exercise/Test exercise: 1, 2

Vocabulary

Ensure that you know all the vocabulary to date.

Section Three

Section 3A

p.144 *is ea id*

The demonstrative pronoun *is ea id* comes in at this point to join your growing collection of these highly useful and versatile words in the Latin lexicon. For example, *is ea id* can feature prominently (although not in the nominative form) in the accusative-and-infinitive (indirect statement) construction which you will learn about in Section Four.

pp.145–8 Comparative and superlative adjectives

Even when these are irregular, they should not hold too many fears for you. In fact, the English derivatives are very helpful memory aids for these forms. You will see from *GVE* that the comparative and superlative forms of *bonus*, *malus* and *magnus* have obviously influenced English vocabulary. Latin derivatives have a wide European net – just one example, the Spanish *mejor* meaning 'better' is clearly related to the comparative of *bonus*, *melior*.

The Reading exercise on p.149 is a splendid reinforcer for the forms of the comparatives and superlatives and it also reminds you of the use of *quam* as described on p.146, note 4. Keep to the same case for both nouns when using *quam* in the comparison of two things, persons.

Exercises

p.145 Exercises: 3–6
pp.148–9 Exercises: 1–3
p.150 Reading exercise/Test exercise

Vocabulary

Ensure that you know all the vocabulary to date.

Section 3B

p.155

Please note that there is a mistake in *GVE* on the bottom line of p.155. It should read 2nd *conj.* verb.

p.158 The perfect participle deponent

This part of speech deserves to be introduced in a slightly less perfunctory manner than you will find in *GVE*. The beauty of the deponent verb's past (or perfect) participle is the fact that it has an active meaning. A non-deponent verb's perfect participle can only have a passive meaning. For instance, *amatus* from *amo* can be translated only as 'having *been* loved', never as '*having* loved'. *Vocatus* means 'having been called' not 'having called', and so on.

For this reason, when translating from Latin to English in future sections, be clear about what type of verb you are dealing with; deponent or non-deponent. In Section 3B you are practising the use of the deponent exclusively, so things at this stage are relatively simple.

You'll get a firm grasp of the participle if you remember that it is a hybrid, combining the function of both a verb and an adjective. The participle tells us something more about a noun or a pronoun expressed or understood; it adds to our information about that noun. So, the participle as adjective can qualify a person, a place, a thing, or even a feeling. For example, consider the following sentence:

> Sorrow, having besieged (attacked) the soul, grows daily.

In Latin using a deponent participle with its active force, this would translate as:

> *Tristitia animum aggressa* [from *aggredior* = I attack] *crescit in dies.*

Although the participle has to behave like an adjective and agree with the noun *tristitia* (hence *aggressa* in agreement with *tristitia* is nominative feminine singular), it is actually telling us about an action performed by sorrow, and this is where the verb (*adgredior*) comes in. By the way, you may find *adgredior, adgressus* written as *aggredior, aggressus* in dictionaries and texts. It is certainly easier to pronounce if we dispense with the '*d*', and the written '*gg*' highlights its relationship with the English words *aggression, aggressive.*

Handy hints about participles generally

Just to consider further the meticulousness of Latin (as the educated writers and grammarians of the language practised it) and the more relaxed attitude to usage in English, read the following pithy paragraph from a Greek language course. You may find the humour rather *passé*, but the point is made memorably, nevertheless.

> We don't think much of participles in English. We have only two worthy of the name. There is the present participle – 'He paused with his hand on the door, *musing* a-while' or the past participle – 'There's that *cursed* knocker again!' We may consider the present participle to be active and the past to be passive. But we are abominably casual about the time of our participles. We may have to use our discretion in order to find out the time of an action referred to in a participle. Look at these:
>
> 1 He went out, crying bitterly.
>
> 2 Saying 'Bah!' she swept out.
>
> In the first sentence we may have a moist trail of evidence to prove that the exit and the tears were simultaneous. But nobody imagines in the second that the lady's departure was accompanied by a prolonged and continuous 'Bah!' like a benighted sheep with a faulty sound box. Yet there is nothing in the form of these two participles to suggest that their times, relative to that of the main verb, are different.
>
> (Kinchin Smith and Melluish, 1951, pp.90–91)

Exercises

pp.157–8	Exercises: 2–5
p.158	Exercises: 1–2
p.160	Exercises: 1–3
p.162	Exercises
pp.162–3	Reading
pp.163–4	Reading exercise/Test exercise
p.164	English–Latin

Vocabulary

Ensure that you know all the vocabulary to date.

Reference

Kinchin Smith, F. and Melluish, T.W. (eds) (1951) *Kepos – Greek in Two Years*, English Universities Press.

Figure 6 Grand cameo of Sainte Chappell Bibliothèque Nationale de France, Cabinet des Medailles. Photograph: Giraudon.

Section 3C

Once you have conquered the concept of the participle and can appreciate the beauty of its economy, the time sequence of the participle is not really very complicated to work out. The economy of the participle is interesting because English has to become rather wordy to express the future participle in Latin. We have to resort to 'about to do', 'on the verge of doing' or something equally cumbersome. 'Going to do' is often the best way to render the future participle.

pp.168–71

The perfect participle passive, which completes the set, is often the easiest to remember because it is frequently the basis of an English derivative. Similarly, the deponent form *aggressus* above gave us 'aggressive'. *GVE* does draw your attention to this fact on p.177.

Cast your eye down the list of perfect participles on pp.169–70 of *GVE* and you'll probably recognize several familiar words. Of course, etymology works both ways, and you can work out the meaning of certain items of English vocabulary from a knowledge of Latin. For example, the verb 'to urinate' in Latin has the following principal parts: *mingo mingere minxi mictus*. You can impress the medical profession with your knowledge of the technical term for passing water, *micturition*, if you are acquainted with this particular Latin verb.

Exercises

If you did the Reading exercise/Test exercise on pp.163–4 you will have noticed that the translation in the Answers section of this Study Guide offers a very literal rendering of the Latin participle constructions. You might wish to try putting the piece in more natural-sounding and idiomatic English now, avoiding so many 'having done' constructions.

Exercises

p.172 Exercises: 1–3
p.173 Exercises: 2
pp.174–5 Exercises: 1, 2, 5
p.175 Reading exercise/Test exercise (N.B. In line 4, the second *seruo* should not be there.)

Vocabulary

Ensure that you know all the vocabulary to date.

Section 3D

p.180

Please note that *obsto* in the running vocabulary (*GVE* p.180) should be conjugation 1.

pp.181–3 The dative

You meet several more functions of the dative case in this section. The ethic dative is not something you are likely to encounter often in your early reading of Latin, if at all. It's useful to be aware of it, but more important, at this stage, that you learn to recognize the dative as the case ending for the indirect object, the possessive dative, and verbs which invariably take a dative case (as listed on *GVE* pp.182–3).

The predicative dative is a succinct expression which can encompass the notion of purpose as *GVE* suggests. But remind yourself of the meaning of 'predicative' on *GVE* p.xxi. It's important not to invest the term 'predicative' with notions of intentionality. It is much closer to the idea of the predicate in English grammar. The predicate is whatever follows the subject of an English sentence and completes our information about that subject. The Latin predicative dative is often best converted into understandable English by the use of words such as 'the object of', 'the source of', 'a means of'.

There are a number of easily learned set phrases involving the predicative dative. *GVE* has not revealed all of them on p.183, so additional phrases that you will find useful to learn are listed below.

admirationi esse	to be an object of amazement to, to amaze (plus the dative of the person amazed – until you get used to the predicative dative the doubling up of the datives can be a bit bemusing)
auxilio esse	to be a means of assistance to, to help
bono esse	to be a source of benefit, to benefit
curae esse	to be a matter of concern, to cause anxiety
decori esse	to bring distinction, to adorn (remember *decus* neuter noun, genitive *decoris* combined with *tutamen* on the rim of the one pound coin and translated as 'ornament and protection')
dedecori esse	to be a cause of shame, to disgrace
dolori esse	to be a cause of grief, to distress
exemplo esse	to be an example

exitio esse	to bring destruction, to ruin
honori esse	to be an honour
impedimento esse	to be a hindrance, to hinder
laudi esse	to be a credit
ludibrio esse	to be an object of ridicule, to be laughed at
odio esse	to be an object of hatred, to be hated
oneri esse	to be a burden, to weigh down
periculo esse	to be a source of danger, to endanger
praesidio esse	to be a means of protection, to protect
saluti esse	to be the salvation, to save
subsidio esse	to be of assistance to, to support, to help
usui esse	to be of use, to benefit
uoluptati esse	to be a source of pleasure to, to please

Exercises

pp.183–4 Revision exercises: 1, 3 (N.B. *All* 1st and 2nd declension dative plurals end in *-is* (except *deabus*, *filiabus*); and *all* 3rd, 4th and 5th declension dative plurals end in *-bus*.)

pp.184–5 Exercises (For question 2, look at *GVE* p.183 on the predicative dative.)

pp.185–6 Reading exercise/Test exercise

Vocabulary

Ensure that you know all the vocabulary to date.

Section Four

There is a lot to learn in Section Four, so do not skimp on the exercises in this final stage. Of course, recognizing the new endings continues to be a vital part of your study but later in this section you will need to concentrate particularly on the grammatical concepts involved in the subjunctive mood.

The final assignment for this course will cover the *whole* of Section Four, *including* the subjunctive, so you should be sure to work through all of the material.

Please note, however, that the examination will test your understanding and linguistic skills up to Section 4D only. You will *not* need to use the subjunctive in the exam.

Figure 7 Cicero. Museo Vaticano, Rome. Photograph: Alinari.

Section 4A

pp.194–6 The imperfect tense

The imperfect tense, expressing incompleted actions in the past, is another conjugation and another example of how precise (punctual) Latin is with its timings, making finer distinctions than English does. The imperfect tense has another set of straightforward endings. There are no variants here but just remember you are attaching the endings to the present stem of the verb, the first principal part, not to the perfect or to the participle.

pp.201–3 Indirect speech in Latin

The accusative-and-infinitive construction expresses something reported or perceived. It may seem a little odd at first but once you have understood the basic formula it is not difficult to recognize or to translate.

Consider the following sentence:

> They say this.

It is clear that the word 'this' is the object of 'they say', answering the question, 'What do they say?'. Suppose that we were given more information, exactly what they said in answer to the question above. The answer might be:

> They say that Caesar is a good man.

The phrase 'that Caesar is a good man' should still be regarded as the object of the verb. That's why you should expect to find the accusative case somewhere in the construction. We can imitate the Latin construction in this particular example, but need to modify the verb slightly for an idiomatic English sound:

> They declare [say] Caesar to be a good man.

Now look at the Latin:

> *dicunt Caesarem esse uirum bonum.*

Hold on to the fact that the subject of what was the original direct statement, 'Caesar is a good man', has to become the object because the whole subordinate clause is the object of the main verb (they say/ *dicunt*) in this new extended sentence.

A second important point concerns the verb and once again is a matter of time-telling. The infinitive form used has to correspond in time or tense to the tense of the original statement. The simple rule of thumb is that the *perfect infinitive* indicates action before the time of the main verb, the *present infinitive* indicates action at the same time as the main verb, and the *future infinitive* indicates action after the time of the main verb.

You may notice in the examples given on *GVE* p.202 that English needs to keep a past tense in the indirect statement when the tense of the main verb is in the past tense. However, Latin uses the present infinitive in the same situation. *Caesar dixit Romam se uenire* translates as 'Caesar said that he *was* coming to Rome'. Latin uses *uenire*, the present infinitive, 'to come', as if the translation were '*is* coming', because the present tense is the one Caesar would have used: original statement, 'I *am* coming to Rome'.

Exercises

The English–Latin exercise starting at the bottom of p.206 will be a test of your understanding but do note that in sentence (b) – 'Cicero said that the slaves entered the temple' – the more natural English would be: 'Cicero said that the slaves had entered the temple'. When translating this remember that the original words of Caesar's were: 'The slaves have entered the temple'. So what tense of the infinitive are you going to use?

Exercises

p.196	Exercises: 2, 4, 5
p.201	Exercises: 2, 4
pp.203–4	Exercises: 1–2*
p.205	Reading exercises: 2
p.206	Reading exercise/Test exercise
p.206	English–Latin

*N.B. The Latin is quoted incorrectly in this question and should read: *homo sum: humani nil a me alienum puto.*

Vocabulary

Ensure that you know all the vocabulary to date.

Section 4B

pp.213–5 The ablative

Section 4B provides plenty of practice on the various uses of the ablative case. Do take notice of *GVE*'s reminder about making comparisons, the first point in 100B (p.214), and the way a comparison works using the ablative instead of *quam*. You might find it slightly confusing that *GVE* illustrates the ablative expressing measure of difference in two sentences with comparative *quam* (point 5).

p.216 Pronouns and adjectives

Now is a good time to remind yourself of how pronouns and pronominal adjectives decline and how we might translate them, especially the ones you meet earlier, where quite delicate nuances of meaning distinguish them.

Exercises

p.216	Exercises: 1(b), (c)
p.218	Exercises: 2
p.219	Exercises: 3

Vocabulary

Ensure that you know all the vocabulary to date.

Section 4C

pp.227–8 The pluperfect

The pluperfect tense is a stage further back in the past than the perfect. *GVE* gives you its full designation as the 'pluperfect indicative active'. The first word, pluperfect, signifies the tense, and the last word, active, is self-evident. Indicative describes the mood of the verb, and as the definition of the word on *GVE* p.xx explains, it suggests definite, actual action.

The only moods of the verb you have met so far are the indicative and the imperative (command form). You are now ready to move on and think about the subjunctive mood, a mood which deals with the hypothetical and unfulfilled, rather than the real, the actual. You will meet the subjunctive in Section 4E but a summary at this point will complete your understanding of the verb conjugation's triple designation.

'Subjunctive' comes from the Latin *subiungo* and denotes something that is joined on; for instance, 'I am waiting here *in case you should come*'. The subordinate, or joined-on, clause is not referring to an actual arrival but only to the possibility of one. This is a natural place for the use of the subjunctive mood. You may have realized that English is capable of expressing the unfulfilled nature of the event by using 'should come', although 'in case you come' would probably be the regular way of ending the English sentence. Most *sub*ordinate clauses have their verbs in the *sub*junctive, but for the present you can relax, as you are about to meet those relative subordinate clauses which do not need verbs in the subjunctive mood.

p.229 The relative pronoun *qui quae quod*

The relative pronoun *qui* represents an exciting leap in the language as far as any student is concerned. Understanding how it works will enable you to translate and construct more complex sentences in Latin. *GVE* painstakingly explains how the relative clause works. Just remember that a relative pronoun has the same gender and number as the noun that it is replacing in the subordinate clause, but its case depends on the grammar of its own clause and is completely independent of the case of the original noun.

If it helps, try separating out the two pieces of information you are likely to be receiving in the sentence. Taking *GVE*'s example from 5(b) on p.230, you could convert the sentence 'Diodorus, whom Verres hated, was afraid' into 'Diodorus was afraid. Verres hated Diodorus'. The Latin would be *Diodorus timebat. Verres Diodorum oderat.* Now simply replace *Diodorum* with the matching relative pronoun – laborious, perhaps, but it should get the right result if you are still in doubt about the correct case of the relative.

pp.232–3 The ablative absolute

The ablative absolute construction is exceedingly common in Latin. If you would like to know more about the ablative absolute, and its exciting possibilities, you can read the short summary below. However, *GVE* does not take the construction this far until Section 5B. This construction is extremely useful for conveying attendant circumstances and can denote temporal and causal relationships between two events. Grammar books frequently discuss the ablative absolute in the context of the participle and its use. The ablative absolute can be used where English would use an active past participle. Unless there is an appropriate deponent verb, this is not an option in Latin.

Consider the following English sentence:

> Having praised the slaves, the man cursed his friends.

The Latin for praise, *laudo*, has no active past participle – *laudatus* attached to *vir* (man) would mean 'the man having been praised'. One way around this, if we want to use a participial phrase, is to go for the ablative absolute construction:

> *servis laudatis, vir amicos vituperavit.*

This literally translates as:

> With the slaves having been praised, the man cursed his friends.

However it would be perfectly legitimate to translate the sentence back into the original English that we started with above, or to say: 'Although the man praised the slaves, he cursed his friends' or 'After the man had praised the slaves, he cursed his friends'.

Just remember that the 'absolute' part of the phrase 'ablative absolute' is all about disconnecting (or 'absolving') the construction from the rest of the sentence grammatically: *absoluo* means 'I loosen'.

p.233 The locative

The locative case had a fleeting mention in the Monty Python sketch recorded on Band 3 of the audio-cassette, but although John Cleese and Graham Chapman arrived at the correct phrasing, *Romani, ite domum,* for 'Romans go home', *domum* is not a locative but the accusative of motion towards a place. *Domi,* the true locative form, is to be translated as 'at home'.

Exercises

Questions 4 and 5 of the exercises on p.229 cover a range of tenses, so if you complete them, you will have done some valuable revision of all the manifestations of the verb in its indicative mood.

p.229 Exercises: 3–5
p.231 Exercises: 1
p.235 Reading exercise/Test exercise

Vocabulary

Ensure that you know all the vocabulary to date.

Section 4D

pp.243–9 The passive

The good news in this section is that all the forms set out on pp.244–6 are familiar ones. You have learned them as endings for the deponent verbs. So, your main task here, as well as refreshing your memory about the conjugation patterns, is to grasp the concept of the passive.

In the sentence 'Tom hit the ball', you could think of the action of the verb going from left to right. The form of the verb is active and the subject acts upon the object. In the sentence 'The ball was hit by Tom' the action of the verb goes from right to left. It is the subject of the verb which receives or suffers the action of the verb. A verb which does not take a direct object cannot be used in a passive construction with an agent performing the action.

Don't worry about the rather fine distinction *GVE* makes in point 2 of the notes on p.249. Most of the time, the human agent needs to be translated with *ab* or *a* plus the ablative, and only inanimate agents dispense with the preposition.

Exercises

pp.247–8	Exercises: 1–2
p.250	Exercises: 2, 4, 5
p.251	Reading exercise/Test exercise

Vocabulary

Ensure that you know all the vocabulary to date.

Section 4E

pp.261–2 Present participles

Remind yourself of the definition of 'predicative' on *GVE* p.xxi. Note 3 on p.262 of *GVE* is the third occasion that a predicative use is mentioned. Do not imagine that there is necessarily any sense of purpose in the function of the present participle. Note, too, that the present participle is always active and is the meeting point for active and deponent verbs with regard to both appearance and role in a sentence; i.e. active verb and deponent verb present participles look and act exactly the same.

As the use of a present participle assumes that the action described in it takes place at the same time as the main verb, you should expect to find it even when the main verb is in the past tense, as the examples below demonstrate.

> *lupum in siluam intrantem conspicimus.*
> We catch sight of a wolf going into the wood.
>
> *lupum in siluam intrantem conspeximus.*
> We caught sight of a wolf going into the wood.
>
> *lupum agnum sequentem conspicimus.*
> We catch sight of a wolf following a lamb.
>
> *lupum agnum sequentem conspeximus.*
> We caught sight of a wolf following a lamb.

You might object that the last two sentences could technically be translated as 'the lamb following the wolf'. This is the sort of situation when common sense and *GVE*'s advice about translating as you go, at least on a first-sight reading, should produce the logical English version.

pp.263–5 Meeting the subjunctive

Unlike your previous experience where you started with the present tense, you are asked to familiarize yourself first with the past (pluperfect) endings of this mood of the verb. This is because it enables you to use the most appropriate tense of the subjunctive to construct some straightforward subordinate clauses where the subjunctive mood is required. The construction with *cum*, meaning 'since' or 'although', always takes the subjunctive.

Exercises

pp.262–3 Exercises: 1–3
pp.265–6 Exercises: 1–2

Vocabulary

Ensure that you know all the vocabulary to date.

Figure 8 Stone copy of the Clupeus Virtutis found in the Cryptoporticus at Arles Musée de l'Arles Antique. Photograph: Michel Lacanaud.

Section 4F

Generally, you should think of the subjunctive as the *tentative* mood. As you learn about the circumstances in which it should be used, this guideline should become clearer. The indirect command, for instance, introduced on pp.279–80, demonstrates the point in so far as an order does not necessarily result in an action. In example (a) at the bottom of p.279, although it is not likely that Caesar's orders were ignored we cannot assume that an action automatically followed, so we are still in the realm of the hypothetical. The translation *GVE* suggests has that revealing word 'should' in the English, which can help us to distinguish between the actual and the ideal. The list on *GVE* p.280 shows that all these verbs taking a subjunctive construction deal with strong wishes, psychological coercion, and command, but, even so, none can guarantee the outcome.

Exercises

p.279	Exercises: 1–2
p.281	Exercises: 1–2
p.282	Exercises: 1–2

Vocabulary

Ensure that you know all the vocabulary to date.

Section 4G

pp.291–2 Conditionals with subjunctive verbs

The *GVE* heading for this section may be misleading in that you will sometimes find 'if' clause constructions which do not need a subjunctive mood. These are known as 'open conditions' and they deal with statements that are non-controversial in an ethical or legal sense.

Below are examples of this sort of straightforward condition; the key distinction between these statements and the ideal or unreal conditions that require the subjunctive mood is that the action or state described in the subordinate clause is assumed to occur and therefore justifies the statement in the main clause.

Si hoc facis, peccas.
If you do this, you do wrong. [*pecco* = first conjugation]

si hoc fecisti, peccauisti.
If you did this, you did wrong.

si hoc facies, peccabis.
If you are going to do this, you will be doing wrong. [Both verbs in future indicative]

(You might raise the objection in this last example that there is no way of knowing if either action is to be carried out! It's not surprising, perhaps, that some future endings can look rather like subjunctive ones. You will just have to accept that the example using the conditional in the future, still has an air of definiteness in it as far as the result of the action is concerned.)

si hoc feceris, poenas dabis.
If you do [literally, if you will have done – future perfect indicative] this, you will pay the penalty.

(Note how exact Latin is about the first action, the 'doing this', which has to happen before the penalty is carried out, even though both actions are taking place in the future; the future perfect, *feceris* is therefore used to keep the sequence of events clear.)

With all these statements there is no room for doubt or negotiation. The *GVE* examples of unreal conditions on p.291 emphasize the difference quite forcefully. For instance, consider the first example from that page.

If I were rich [add on 'which I'm not'] I would not be working now [add on 'but I am'].

These two manufactured asides (assumptions) demonstrate that the state described is not the reality of the situation. So, you can see that the subjunctive has to play its part.

Which tense?

The rules are summarized by *GVE* on the same page. As you learned the pluperfect subjunctive first, you may as well know about the use of pluperfect subjunctive in conditional clauses. It completes the pattern of unreal conditions for you and is probably the easiest to handle as it straightforwardly translates with the auxiliary 'had' in English.

si canis latravisset, furem cepissimus.
If the dog had barked, we would have caught the thief.

(The awkward but grammatically correct English for *furem cepissimus* would be: 'we had caught the thief'.)

So, remember:

- 'were to ... would' requires the present subjunctive in both clauses;
- 'were (now) ... would (now)' requires the imperfect subjunctive in both;
- 'had ... would have' requires the pluperfect subjunctive in both clauses.

pp.294–5 The subjunctive in reported speech

It may be helpful to bring out a little more explicitly why the subjunctive is needed in the examples *GVE* gives.

It is useful to add the word 'allegedly' when one is dealing with apparently factual statements in reported speech. In the first *GVE* example, remember that he said that everyone loved him because he was handsome. 'Everyone loved him' may well be true but the reason given is only his opinion or speculation.

Exercises

p.292 Exercises: 1–2
pp.297–8 English–Latin

Vocabulary

Ensure that you know all the vocabulary to date.

Postscript

The subjunctive makes an exciting finish to this course because with it, you are moving out of the realms of simple and largely factual narrative to more sophisticated thinking which requires more sophisticated forms of expression. This qualitative leap in your learning, if you complete it successfully, will mean you are much closer to an understanding and reading of the complex Latin sentence.

I was told quite firmly when studying for my classics degree that Latin should be quaffed like beer, not sipped like wine. If you are in the happy position of having plenty of leisure time in the future, the more Latin you can go on to read, the better!

What next?

You should spend the remaining time on the course revising and consolidating your work for the examination. Remember to study the Specimen Examination Paper and consult your tutor if you are in any doubt about what is required. You will also find that the vocabulary lists in the Assignment Booklet will help you to prepare for the examination.

After the course

Although you have covered a great deal of ground in this course, there will, however, still be some way to go before you can tackle continuous Latin in the original. If you would like to continue by working on the rest of *RLT* and *GVE*, you may be interested to know that answers and a translation of the running texts for Section 5 are available to help with informal further study. Please send a large self-addressed envelope marked *RLT Notes* to: The Course Manager, A297, Faculty of Arts, The Open University, Walton Hall, Milton Keynes, MK7 6AA.

Appendix 1:

Answers to Exercises in GVE

Section One

Introduction

p.4 Exercises

1	you (s.) are	*es*
	there are	*sunt*
	he is	*est*
	there is	*est*
	you (pl.) are	*estis*
	they are	*sunt*
	it is	*est*
	I am	*sum*
	she is	*est*

2	*sum*	I am	*sumus*	we are
	sunt	they are	*est*	he is
	estis	you (pl.) are	*es*	you (s.) are
	est	he/she/it is *or* there is	*sunt*	they are *or* there are
	sumus	we are	*sum*	I am
	es	you (s.) are	*estis*	you (pl.) are

p.4 Reading

(a) It is the household.
(b) The slave girl is Staphyla.
(c) For the pot is full of gold.
(d) The cook is a slave.
(e) Phaedra is the daughter.
(f) In the house (there) are Euclio, Phaedra and the slave girl.
(g) The miser is an old man.
(h) Near the river there is a small field.

p.4 English–Latin

(a) There are, in the household, Euclio, Phaedra (and) Staphyla.
est in familia serua.

(b) Euclio and Phaedra are in the house.
serua in aedibus est.

(c) I am Euclio.
es seruus/serua.

(d) Euclio's daughter is Phaedra.
serua Euclionis Staphyla est.

(e) Who are you? (s.)
Euclio sum.

(f) Who are you? (pl.)
Euclio et Phaedra sumus.

Section 1A

p.9 Exercises

1

celo	*timeo*	*porto*	*habeo*
celas	*times*	*portas*	*habes*
celat	*timet*	*portat*	*habet*
celamus	*timemus*	*portamus*	*habemus*
celatis	*timetis*	*portatis*	*habetis*
celant	*timent*	*portant*	*habent*

2

clamas	you (s.) shout	*clamatis*
habent	they have	*habet*
intrat	he enters	*intrant*
uoco	I call	*uocamus*
sumus	we are	*sum*
portamus	we carry	*porto*
times	you (s.) fear	*timetis*
habetis	you (pl.) have	*habes*
est	he is	*sunt*
timet	he fears	*timent*
uocant	they call	*uocat*
celatis	you (pl.) hide	*celas*
timemus	we fear	*timeo*
habeo	I have	*habemus*
sunt	they are	*est*

3

you (pl.) have	*habetis*
I do hide	*celo*
we are carrying	*portamus*
they call	*uocant*
you (s.) are afraid of	*times*
she is dwelling	*habitat*
there are	*sunt*
it has	*habet*
there enters	*intrat*
she is	*est*

p.13 Exercises

1

coquus	*coqui*	*aula*	*aulae*
coque	*coqui*	*aula*	*aulae*
coquum	*coquos*	*aulam*	*aulas*
coqui	*coquorum*	*aulae*	*aularum*
coquo	*coquis*	*aulae*	*aulis*
coquo	*coquis*	*aula*	*aulis*

2

seruarum	gen. pl.
coquo	dat./abl. sing.
coronam	acc. sing.
seruos	acc. pl.
scaenae	gen./dat. sing. *or* nom. pl.
filia	abl. sing. (*filia* nom. sing.)
coquus	nom. sing.
serui	gen. sing. *or* nom. pl.
coquum	acc. sing.
filiae	gen./dat. sing. *or* nom. pl.
scaenas	acc. pl.
seruo	dat./abl. sing.
coquorum	gen. pl.
aula	nom. sing. (*aula* abl. sing.)
seruis	dat./abl. pl.

3

	Translation	Plural/singular
(a)	I am a slave.	*sumus serui.*
(b)	I carry a pot.	*aulas portamus.*
(c)	They have garlands.	*coronam habet.*
(d)	The slave girl fears the slave.	*seruae timent seruos.*
(e)	You call the slave girls.	*seruam uocas.*
(f)	The slave girls carry the pots.	*serua aulam portat.*
(g)	We hide the pots.	*celo aulam.*
(h)	The cooks hide the slave girls.	*seruam celat coquus.*
(i)	The household has a garland.	*familiae coronas habent.*
(j)	The slave calls the slave girl.	*uocant serui seruas.*

If you have made mistakes, first check the endings of the nouns to see whether they are nominative (subject) or accusative (object).

p.14 Exercise

onto the stage	*in scaenam* (acc. because movement towards)
in the pot	*in aula* (abl. because position)
onto the garlands	*in coronas*
into the pots	*in aulas*
in the household	*in familia*
towards the slave woman	*ad seruam*
in the slaves	*in seruis*
towards the daughter	*ad filiam*

pp.15–16 Reading exercise

1 (a) The slave enters (onto) the stage. He (the slave) carries garlands.

(b) The cooks are in the house. They (the cooks) call the slave women.

(c) There is a slave woman in Euclio's household. She (the slave woman) is Staphyla.

(d) Onto the stage enters Demaenetus. He (Demaenetus) has a pot full of gold.

(e) The cook and the slave woman are shouting. For they (the cook and the slave woman) fear the slave.

4 Demaenetus sees the cooks and flute-players. They are coming to his daughter's wedding. They enter the house of Demaenetus and prepare the wedding. Now the house of Demaenetus is full of cooks and flute-players. But Demaenetus is afraid. For he has a pot full of gold. For if the pot full of gold is in Demaenetus' house, Demaenetus is very afraid of thieves. Demaenetus hides the pot. Now the gold is safe. Now Demaenetus is safe. Now the pot is safe. For the Lar has the pot full of gold. Now the pot lies hidden near the Lar under the ground. Therefore Demaenetus now approaches the Lar and prays. 'O Lar, I, Demaenetus, call on you. O protector of my household, I bring to you my pot full of gold. My daughter's wedding is today. But I fear thieves. For my house is full of thieves. I beg and beseech you, protect Demaenetus' pot full of gold.'

p.17 English–Latin

(a) The cook carries Demaenetus' pot.
seruus coronas coquorum habet.

(b) You are shouting but I am carrying the pots.
serua timet. ego igitur coquum uoco.

(c) Why is the stage full of slaves?
cur aedes plenae sunt coquorum?

(d) I, the Lar, call you. Why do you fear me?
ego Phaedra intro. cur aulam celatis?

(e) If he has gold, Demaenetus is afraid.
si aulam celant, serui timent.

(f) It is garlands and pots the slaves are carrying.
coquum et seruam uocat Demaenetus.

Section 1B

p.22 Exercises

1

honor	*honores*
honorem	*honores*
honoris	*honorum*
honori	*honoribus*
honore	*honoribus*
fur	*fures*
furem	*fures*
furis	*furum*
furi	*furibus*
fure	*furibus*

2

Euclionis	gen. sing.
furem	acc. sing.
aedium	gen. pl.
honores	nom. *or* acc. pl.
Lar	nom. sing.
senum	gen. pl.
aedis	acc. pl. (see *GVE* p.20)
honorem	acc. sing.
fur	nom. sing.
Laris	gen. sing.

3 (a) Then the thief sees the old man's treasure.
deinde thesauros senum fures uident.

(b) The Lar does not have honour.
Lares honores non habent.

(c) Therefore the god does not look after the old man.
igitur senes dei non curant.

(d) But why are you praying, old men?
quare tamen supplicas, senex?

(e) At last the old man has the ointment.
unguenta (2nd decl. neuter) *senes tandem possident/habent.*

(f) The old man now lives in the house.
in aedibus senes nunc habitant.

(g) A thief always likes a pot full of gold.
fures aulas auri plenas semper amant. (*gold* is usually singular)

(h) But a thief does not have respect.
honores tamen non habent fures.

(i) Why do you not enter (into) the house, old man?
quare in aedis non intratis, senes?

(j) The old man secretly loves the slave woman.
seruas clam amant senes.

p.24 Exercises

2 **Genitive plurals**

honorum	from *honor* 3rd decl. masc. = respect
furum	from *fur* 3rd decl. masc. = thief
unguentorum	from *unguentum* 2nd decl. neut. = ointment
senum	from *senex* 3rd decl. masc. = old man

3 **Plural nouns**

ingenia	from *ingenium* 2nd decl. neut. = talents
unguentis	from *unguentum* 2nd decl. neut. = ointments
somnia	from *somnium* 2nd decl. neut. = dreams
pericula	from *periculum* 2nd decl. neut. = dangers

pp.25–6 Exercises

1 *multas curas*
multum aurum
multi or *multos fures* (nom. *or* acc. pl.)
multum senem
multi honoris
multam aedem
multorum seruorum
multorum senum
multas aedis (acc. pl.)
multae coronae (gen./dat. sing. *or* nom. pl.)

2

multus	(masc. nom. sing.)	*senex, seruus*
multi	(masc/neut. gen. sing. *or* masc. nom. pl.)	*Laris, senes, serui*
multis	(masc./fem./neut. dat./abl. pl.)	*honoribus, senibus*
multas	(fem. acc. pl.)	*aedis, familias*
multae	(fem. gen./dat. sing. *or* nom. pl.)	*seruae, aedi*
multa	(fem. nom. sing. *or* neut. nom./acc. pl.)	*unguenta, cura*

3

many slave girls	*multae seruae*
of much respect	*multi honoris*
of many garlands	*multarum coronarum*
much gold	*multum aurum*
many an old man	*multum senem*
of many thieves	*multorum furum*
many old men	*multos senes*

If you have made any mistakes in the last three exercises, check the gender and declension of the noun.

4 (a) Many thieves are in the house.
(b) Many old men have many cares.
(c) Many slave girls are full of cares.
(d) Euclio has much gold (and) many pots full of gold.
(e) The old man has many slaves.

5 (a) No power is long-lived.
(b) Life is neither a good nor a bad thing.
(c) Nobility is the only unparalleled goodness.
(d) Life is long if it is full.
(e) Fortune is blind.

p.28 Reading exercises

2 (a) *clamant* is plural; *serui, senex, seruae* are all subjects.
The slaves, the old man and the slave girls are all shouting.
(b) *dat* is singular; *multum honorem* is the object, *Phaedra* is the subject.
Therefore Phaedra gives much respect.
(c) *possidet* is singular; *Lar* is the subject, *aedis* is the object.
Now the Lar possesses the house.

(d) *amant* is plural; *di* is the subject, *multum honorem* is the object.
The gods like much respect.

(e) *dat* is singular; *aurum* is the subject (N.B. neuter noun), *multas curas* is the object.
Gold gives many worries.

(f) *habitant* is plural; *serui* is the subject.
Slaves also live in the house.

(g) *est* is singular; *aurum* is the subject.
There is much gold in the pot.

(h) *timent* is plural; *fures* is subject *or* object, *senes* is subject *or* object, *multi* must be subject.
Either: However, many thieves fear old men.
Or (better sense): However, many old men fear thieves.

(i) *intrant* is plural; *senex* and *seruus* are both subject.
Why are the old man and the slave entering (onto) the stage?

(j) *explicat* is singular; *Lar* is the subject, *curas* is the object.
At last the Lar explains the old man's worries.

p.29 Reading exercise/Test exercise

The Lar enters (onto) the stage. He is the god of Euclio's household. The Lar protects Demaenetus' treasure under the earth. Much treasure is in a pot. But Euclio does not know about the treasure because he does not look after the Lar. For he gives (him) no ointment, no garlands (and) no respect. But the Lar likes Phaedra, the daughter of the greedy old man. For Euclio's daughter gives (him) much ointment, many garlands (and) much respect. Therefore the Lar gives Demaenetus' pot to Euclio, because Euclio's daughter is good. But Euclio places the pot under the earth again, because he is greedy (a miser). For Euclio fears thieves very much! He has many worries! The treasure bothers the greedy and worried old man. For the house(s) of the rich men are full of thieves.

Section 1C

Exercises p.37

1 *time, timete*
roga, rogate
tace, tacete
cogita, cogitate
mone, monete
cura, curate
posside, possidete

2 give a garland!
carry water!
stay in the house!
be quiet!
guard the treasure!
warn (your) daughter!

3 *uidete!*
roga Euclionem!
tacete!
celate aulam!

p.38 Exercises

1	*i*	go (sing.)	*ite*
	eunt	they go	*it*
	itis	you (pl.) go	*is*
	eo	I go	*imus*
	it	he/she/it goes	*eunt*
	imus	we go	*eo*
	exitis	you (pl.) go out	*exis*
	abimus	we go away	*abeo*
	abitis	you (pl.) go away	*abis*
	redeunt	they return	*redit*
	reditis	you (pl.) return	*redis*
	ite	go (pl.)	*i*
	redeo	I return	*redimus*
	exeunt	they go out	*exit*

2 *abimus*
redeunt
abi
aditis
exit
eo
redite
is

p.39 Exercises

1	*meo, tuo igne*	abl. sing.
	meas, tuas aedis	acc. pl.
	mei, tui honoris,	gen. sing.
	mea, tua familia	abl. sing.
	meorum, tuorum oculorum	gen. pl.
	meo, tuo domino	dat./abl. sing.
	meae, tuae aquae	gen./dat. sing., nom. pl.
	meum, tuum, Euclionem	acc. sing.
	meus, tuus senex	nom. sing.
2	*misero Euclioni*	dat. sing.
	misera Phaedra	abl. sing.
	miser deus	nom. sing.
	miseram filiam	acc. sing.
	miseris aedibus	dat./abl. pl.
	miseri domini	gen. sing. *or* nom. pl.
	miserarum seruarum	gen. pl.
	miseris coquis	dat./abl. pl.
	miserorum senum	gen. pl.

p.40 Exercises

1 (a) Neither slave girls nor slaves stay in my master's house.
manet in dominorum meorum aedibus neque serua neque seruus.
N.B. *aedes*, when it means 'house', is plural.

(b) The wicked old man's wicked slave girl is annoying my master.
malorum senum malae seruae dominos meos uexant.

(c) Your neighbour sees my neighbour.
tui uicini uicinos meos uident.

(d) The poor old man's slave never stays in the house.
senum miserorum serui in aedibus numquam manent.

(e) The poor slave girls never approach or pray to my Lar.
serua misera ad Lares meos numquam adit neque supplicat.

(f) The wicked master immediately thrashes his slave girls, poor wretches.
domini mali seruam statim uerberant miseram.

2 (a) *malus* – nom. masc. sing. = *senex*
multum – acc. masc. sing. = *honorem*
The wicked old man does therefore not have much respect.

(b) *mea* – abl. fem. sing. = *aula*
tuus – nom. masc. sing. = *ignis*
Your fire is in my pot.

(c) *meis* – dat./abl. fem. pl. = *aedibus*
multi – nom. masc. pl. = *patres*
In my house, however, live many fathers.

(d) *malos* – acc. masc. pl. = *senes*
meus – nom. masc. sing. = *Lar*
For my Lar does not like wicked old men.

(e) *meus* – nom. masc. sing. = *pater*
tuum – acc. masc. sing. = *ignem*
Does my father keep your fire safe?

3 (a) Money alone reigns.

(b) The truth never dies.

(c) A greedy man is always in need.

(d) Death does not frighten a wise man off.

(e) Death in a rout is disgraceful, but death in a victory is glorious.

p.41 Exercise

ex aqua
in oculum
ab igne
ad dominos
ab aedibus
in scaenam

p.41 Reading exercises

1	(a)	*timet*	The poor old man is afraid of his neighbour.
	(b)	*celat*	For my master is hiding your fire.
	(c)	*amas*	I do not like my slave and you do not like yours.
	(d)	*uerberant*	Then the wicked slaves beat me.
	(e)	*uocat*	My neighbour calls the wicked slaves.
	(f)	*portat*	The wicked slave girl, my dear master, is carrying the pot.
	(g)	*moneo*	I also warn the poor thief.
	(h)	*do*	You are giving fire, I, water.
	(i)	*uexat*	Your slave girl always troubles my eyes.
	(j)	*possidet*	Why does poor Euclio never possess gold, ointment and garlands?

p.42 Reading exercise/Test exercise

EUCLIO (*SHOUTING*): Get out! Get out of the house, slave girl.

The slave girl comes on to the stage.

SLAVE GIRL: What is it, my dear master? Why are you calling me out of the house? (*Euclio thrashes the slave girl.*) O poor me. How my master annoys me, for now he is thrashing me. But why are you thrashing me, master?

EUCLIO: O dear me. Be quiet. How wicked you are! How you annoy poor old me! Stay there, Staphyla, stay put. Don't move. I'm warning you.

Euclio goes into the house.

SLAVE GIRL: O dear me. How unhappy my master is.

Euclio comes out of the house on to the stage.

EUCLIO: It's safe. But why are you standing there? Why are you not going into the house? Go away! Go into the house! Close the door! (*The slave girl goes into the house.*) Now I'm going off to the praetor, because I'm a poor old man. How unwillingly I go! But if I stay here, my neighbours* say 'Aha! The wretched old man has a lot of money'.

* You may feel you want to say 'will say' here, but you have not yet met the future tense.

pp.42–3 English–Latin

(a) Staphyla, go away and carry water!
seruae, exite et ignem rogate!

(b) However, as for you, my master, why do you have wicked worries?
tu autem, mi Euclio, quare seruam miseram amas?

(c) How a lot of gold worries wretched old men!
ut malus senex seruos uerberat miseros!

(d) O dear me! How my eyes trouble me!
o me miserum! ut miser senex sum!

(e) Wicked are the masters unhappy slaves have.
miserum senem misera filia amat.

(f) The eyes of the wicked slaves do not see the worries of the unhappy master.
malae seruae oculi filiae miserae curam non uident.

Section 1D

p.48 Exercises

1 *dicit*
ducunt
audimus
dicimus
auditis
dic!
audite!
ducite!
dicis
audit
audiunt

2

2	*curo*	1	I look after
	celat	1	he/she hides
	habetis	2	you (pl.) have
	ducunt	3	they lead
	rogas	1	you ask
	possidemus	2	we possess
	audio	4	I hear

3

3	you (pl.) say	*dicis*
	they hear	*audit*
	we make prayers to	*supplico*
	you (s.) hear	*auditis*
	I say	*dicimus*
	we lead	*duco*
	we hear	*audio*
	they shout	*clamat*
	you (s.) are silent	*tacetis*

p.50 Exercises

1	*nomen*	*magnum, miserum, pulchrum*
	nominis	*magni, miseri, pulchri*
	nomine	*magno, misero, pulchro*
	nomina	*magna, misera, pulchra*
	nominum	*magnorum, miserorum, pulchrorum*
2	*uxorum*	*pulchrarum miserarum*
	sororibus	*pulchris miseris*
	uiro	*pulchro misero*
	uxoris	*pulchrae miserae*
	feminae	*pulchrae miserae*
	fratri	*pulchro misero*
	aedis	*pulchras miseras*
	Larem	*pulchrum miserum*
	serua	*pulchra misera*
	aedes	*pulchrae miserae*
	feminis	*pulchris miseris*
	domini	*pulchri miseri*
	seruos	*pulchros miseros*

p.51 Exercises

1	(a)	*cuius*	
	(b)	*quas*	feminas
	(c)	*quid*	
	(d)	*quod*	nomen
	(e)	*quem*	
	(f)	*cuius*	feminae
	(g)	*quam*	
	(h)	*qui*	uir

pp.52–3 Exercises

1 (a) *multam* – acc. fem. sing. = *pecuniam*
Excellent wives do not possess a lot of money.
(b) *multi* – nom. masc. pl. = *filii*
Many sons love my sisters.
(c) *optimi* – nom. masc. pl. = *senes*
Excellent old men do not annoy wretched slaves.
(d) *pulchras* – acc. fem. pl. = *sorores*
Wicked brothers beat their beautiful sisters.
(e) *multi* – nom. masc. pl. = *senes*
Many old men take beautiful women home (*or* marry them).

2 into the house
in the pot
towards the Lar
from the fires
into the water
out of the pots
in the house
in the water
from the master/by the master
out of the eyes

3 *in aedibus*
ad puellam
ad fratres
ab uxore
in scaenam
in aedibus (this is a misprint, a repetition of the first phrase of this question)
ex aqua
ab ignibus

4 too many garlands
enough slaves
too much water
enough names
too many sisters
enough fire

5 (a) What man do I hear?
(b) Whose name are you now saying?
(c) There is always enough gold in Euclio's house.
(d) Euclio's unhappy daughter has too many cares.
(e) As for you, however, which woman are you taking home (marrying)?

6 (a) Who is a good man?
(b) Who is not terrified of poverty?
(c) Who hides his love well?
(d) What is a happy life? Freedom from worry and continual peace.
(e) What is death? Either the end or a transition.
(f) Unrestrained anger produces madness.
(g) Fate controls our life, not wisdom.

p.53 Reading

1	(a)	*habet*	At last the man considers me his son.
	(b)	*habet*	Euclio considers his neighbour rich.
	(c)	*faciunt*	*You could choose any person of the verb because the subject is not specified, e.g.* They make Euclio poor.
	(d)	*facit*	Megadorus makes Euclio's daughter his wife.
	(e)	*habeo*	I, however, consider rich men unfortunate.
	(f)	*facit*	The master makes wicked slaves unhappy.

p.54 Reading exercise/Test exercise

Eunomia, his sister, calls Megadorus, a rich man and Euclio's neighbour, out of the house. For Eunomia is worried, because Megadorus does not have a wife. Megadorus, however, does not want a wife. For wives make rich men poor. Megadorus has enough gold and does not like pretty women. For when a woman is pretty, so she annoys her husband. Just as a man is rich, in the same way his wife makes him a poor man. However Megadorus considers Eunomia an excellent sister. When, therefore, his sister makes demands, her brother acts accordingly. For he considers Phaedra, Euclio's daughter, an excellent girl. However, as Euclio is a poor man, so Phaedra has no dowry. Megadorus, however, does not want a dowry. For if wives are rich and have a large dowry, great is the expense after the wedding, and the husbands give too much money.

p.54–5 English–Latin

(a) As I am an excellent sister, so you are an excellent brother.
ut Phaedra optima filia est, ita Euclio pater optimus.

(b) My master considers his brother an excellent man.
pulchras feminas uxores malas habeo.

(c) What is the name of your wife?
quis frater uicini est mei?

(d) A poor man marries a poor wife.
optimi uiri pulchras uxores domum ducunt.

(e) The women are standing in the house.
puellae in aquam eunt.

(f) I have enough gold and enough money.
nimis diues pecuniae habet, nimis curae.

Section 1E

p.60 Exercises

1 *facis*
audite!
ferunt
fer/duc
uult
facimus
fert
ite!
uis
posce!
facio
cape dotem

2	*facimus*	we make	1st pers. pl.	*facio*
	fert	he brings	3rd pers. sing.	*ferunt*
	uult	he wishes	3rd pers. sing.	*uolunt*
	ferunt	they bring	3rd pers. pl.	*fert*
	dic	say!	sing. imperative	*dicite*
	ferte	bring!	pl. imperative	*fer*
	uolumus	we wish	1st pers. pl.	*uolo*
	est	he is	3rd pers. sing.	*sunt*
	eunt	they go	3rd pers. pl.	*it*
	facis	you make	2nd pers. sing.	*facitis*
	ducite	lead!	pl. imperative	*duc*
	ite	go!	pl. imperative	*i*
	capite	capture!	pl. imperative	*cape*

p.61 Exercises

1	*onus*	nom./acc. sing.	*multum*
	oneris	gen. sing.	*multi*
	onere	abl. sing.	*multo*
	onera	nom./acc. pl.	*multa*
	oneribus	dat./abl. pl.	*multis*

2	*pulchro* (masc./neut., dat./abl. sing.)	*scelere* (neut. abl. sing.)
	pulchra (fem. nom. sing. *or* neut. nom./acc. pl.)	*femina* (fem. nom. sing.) *facinora* (neut. nom./acc. pl.) *scelera* (neut. nom./acc. pl.)
	pulchrum (neut. nom./acc. sing. *or* masc. acc. sing.)	*opus* (neut. nom./acc. sing.) *seruum* (masc. acc. sing.) *Larem* (masc. acc. sing.) *scelus* (neut. nom./acc. sing.)
	pulchrorum (neut./masc. gen. pl.)	*nominum* (neut. gen. pl.) *deorum* (masc. gen. pl.) *scelerum* (neut. gen. pl.)

pp.61–2 Exercise

(a)	*est bona puella.*	She's a good girl.
	estne bona puella?	Is she a good girl?
(b)	*imus ad aedis Euclionis.*	We are going to Euclio's house.
	imusne ad aedis Euclionis?	Are we going to Euclio's house?
(c)	*fert bene onus serua.*	The slave-woman carries the load well.
	fertne bene onus serua?	Does the slave-woman carry the load well?
(d)	*optimum consilium habent.*	They have the best plan.
	optimumne consilium habent?	Do they have the best plan?
(e)	*Euclio filiam statim promittit.*	Euclio promises his daughter at once.
	Euclione filiam statim promittit?	Does Euclio promise his daughter at once?
(f)	*Megadorus satis pecuniae habet.*	Megadorus has enough money.
	Megadorusne satis pecuniae habet?	Does Megadorus have enough money?

(g)	*soror fratrem bene audit.*	The sister listens to her brother well.
	sororne fratrem bene audit?	Does the sister listen to her brother well?
(h)	*scaenam uidetis.*	You see the stage.
	scaenamne uidetis?	Do you see the stage?
(i)	*Euclio honorem numquam dat.*	Euclio never gives respect.
	Euclione honorem numquam dat?	Does Euclio never give respect?
(j)	*uxores nimis auri semper habent.*	Wives always have too much gold.
	uxoresne nimis auri semper habent?	Do wives always have too much gold?

p.62 Exercises

1 into the house
out of the dowry
in mind
towards the men
from the water
out of the fires
at home
out of danger
into death
towards the waters
into danger

2 (a) Where is Megadorus? What plan does he have?
(b) Does the rich man want a beautiful wife? What's the problem?
(c) I therefore consider you to be good men.
(d) The slaves commit too much villainy and too many wicked deeds in the house.
(e) What burden are you carrying? Where are you going to?

3 (a) Hasten slowly. (i.e. more haste, less speed!)
(b) Virtue alone makes life happy.
(c) The wise man does nothing unwillingly.
(d) An author praises his work.
(e) There is no moderation in the mob.
(f) Pleasure is neither a good nor an evil.

p.63 Reading exercises

1 (a) Masc.; refers to Megadorus.
Megadorus marries Euclio's daughter without a dowry. He is therefore an excellent man.
(b) Neut.; refers to the fact given in the first sentence.
At home today, Megadorus neither prepares the marriage-rites nor summons cooks. That is bad.
(c) Fem.; refers to Eunomia.
Eunomia is the sister of Megadorus. She is a good woman.
(d) Neut.; refers to the fact given in the first sentence.
Eunomia has a brother. There is no doubt.
(e) Masc.; refers to Euclio.
Euclio loves his daughter. He is not a bad man.
(f) Neut.; refers to the fact given in the first sentence.
Euclio is afraid. That is not doubtful.
(g) Neut.; refers to *consilium*.
Staphyla hears Euclio's plan. It is a bad one.
(h) Fem.; refers to Staphyla.
Staphyla goes back into the house. For she is full of care.

p.64 Reading exercise/Test exercise

Megadorus sees his neighbour Euclio. Euclio is leaving the forum. He is worried. For Euclio's mind is at home, because he doesn't see his gold, but Euclio himself is outside. Megadorus greets Euclio ingratiatingly, as a rich man greets a poor one. However Euclio is afraid, because Megadorus is a rich man. The reason is obvious. Megadorus wants Euclio's treasure. There is no doubt. Euclio goes into the house, he sees the gold, it is safe. He therefore leaves the house. Megadorus asks for the daughter of Euclio as his wife. Euclio promises his daughter, but without a dowry. For he is a poor man. He therefore has no dowry. Megadorus wants no dowry. He is a good man and rich enough. The marriage-rites are today. Megadorus therefore summons a cook into the house. However Staphyla is afraid, because Phaedra is pregnant by Lyconides. Megadorus marries a pregnant wife. That is a bad thing.

p.64 English–Latin

(a) Are you, a bad man, pouring scorn on me, a very good man?
irridetne Euclionem, homo diues pauperem?

(b) That's bad. For Megadorus is making Euclio's daughter his wife.
non dubium est. senex puellam filiam habet.

(c) Return to the Lar, slaves! Bring many garlands!
i in aedis, serua. fer onera.

(d) What plan is there? Does Megadorus want a dowry? That's bad.
quid noui? pecuniamne uis? non dubium est.

(e) Where are you going to? Are you going into the house? Are you preparing marriage-rites today? That's excellent.
quid uolunt? domumne eunt? oneranе ferunt? boni sunt.

(f) Cheer up, Megadorus. For the plan is a good one.
bonum animum habe, domine. nam factum optimum est.

Section 1F

p.69 Exercise

habere	to have
explicare	to explain
celare	to hide
inuenire	to find
manere	to stay
*redire**	to return
ducere	to lead
dicere	to say
poscere	to demand
stare	to stand
rogare	to ask
fugere	to escape
amittere	to lose
*auferre**	to take away
facere	to make, do
*esse**	to be

* indicates an irregular verb. If you have made any mistakes, check the conjugation of the verb.

pp.71–2 Exercise

1	*puer audax*	*pueri audaces*
	puerum audacem	*pueros audaces/audacis*
	pueri audacis	*puerorum audacium*
	puero audaci	*pueris audacibus*
	puero audaci	*pueris audacibus*
	omnis aqua	*omnes aquae*
	omnem aquam	*omnes aquas*
	omnis aquae	*omnium aquarum*
	omni aquae	*omnibus aquis*
	omni aqua	*omnibus aquis*

ingens periculum	*ingentia pericula*
ingens periculum	*ingentia pericula*
ingentis periculi	*ingentium periculorum*
ingenti periculo	*ingentibus periculis*
ingenti periculo	*ingentibus periculis*

2

Noun	**Case**	**Num.**	**Gend.**	***omnis***	***ingens***	***audax***
seruae	gen.	s.	f.	*omnis*	*ingentis*	*audacis*
	dat.	s.		*omni*	*ingenti*	*audaci*
	nom.	pl.		*omnes*	*ingentes*	*audaces*
thesauri	gen.	s.	m.	*omnis*	*ingentis*	*audacis*
	nom.	pl.		*omnes*	*ingentes*	*audaces*
oculos	acc.	pl.	m.	*omnis(-es)*	*ingentis(-es)*	*audacis(-es)*
dominus	nom.	s.	m.	*omnis*	*ingens*	*audax*
nominibus	dat.	pl.	n.	*omnibus*	*ingentibus*	*audacibus*
	abl.	pl.		*omnibus*	*ingentibus*	*audacibus*
consilium	nom.	s.	n.	*omne*	*ingens*	*audax*
	acc.	s.		*omne*	*ingens*	*audax*
cena	abl.	s.	f.	*omni*	*ingenti*	*audaci*
turbarum	gen.	pl.		*omnium*	*ingentium*	*audacium*
ciui	dat.	s.	m.	*omni*	*ingenti*	*audaci*
pecunias	acc.	pl.	f.	*omnis(-es)*	*ingentis(-es)*	*audacis(-es)*
puella	abl.	s.	f.	*omni*	*ingenti*	*audaci*
periculo	dat.	s.	n.	*omni*	*ingenti*	*audaci*
	abl.	s.		*omni*	*ingenti*	*audaci*
ignis	nom.	s.	m.	*omnis*	*ingens*	*audax*
	gen.	s.		*omnis*	*ingentis*	*audacis*
animis	dat.	pl.	m.	*omnibus*	*ingentibus*	*audacibus*
	abl.	pl.		*omnibus*	*ingentibus*	*audacibus*

3

ingentem	acc. sing. masc./fem.	*deum*	acc. sing. masc.
audax	nom. sing. masc./fem.	*consilium*	nom./acc. sing. neut.
	or nom./acc. sing. neut.	*homo*	nom. sing. masc.
		dominus	nom. sing. masc.
omnium	gen. pl. masc./fem./neut.	*coquorum*	gen. pl. masc.
tristes	nom./acc. pl. masc./fem.	*animos*	acc. pl. masc.
		domini	nom. pl. masc.
		filiae	nom. pl. fem.
facilia	nom./acc./pl. neut.	*scelera*	nom./acc. pl. neut.
difficili	dat./abl. sing.	*coquo*	dat./abl. sing. masc.
	masc./fem./neut.	*filia*	abl. sing. fem.
		exitio	dat./abl. sing. neut.

p.73 Exercises

1 (a) Therefore the bold cook wishes to cook a huge dinner.
(b) Why do you want to know all the names of the cooks?
(c) However you have a bold plan in mind.
(d) When you want to come into the house, call us at once.
(e) Every poor man wants to commit bold crimes.
(f) A huge crowd of bold men is approaching the house of Megadorus.

2 (a) Many women neither sleep nor cook dinner.
(b) He is taking the goods away.
(c) You (pl.) want to know everything.
(d) Handsome men love beautiful women.
(e) Everyone wants to have money.
(f) Many men flee, but many stand firm.
(g) A rich man does not love a poor one.
(h) All good men care for citizens.
(i) Wicked men consider wicked deeds.
(j) Money worries everybody.

3 (a) Every time of life is both short and frail.
(b) Old age is an incurable disease.
(c) Anger is a short madness.

(d) Man is an animal possessing reason.
(e) The way to a happy life is easy.
(f) It is difficult not to write satire.
(g) It is difficult suddenly to lay aside a long-lasting love.
(h) To change nature indeed is difficult.
(i) Woman is a fickle and changeable thing.
(j) An old man who is a soldier is a disgraceful thing; love in an old man is a disgraceful thing.

p.74 Reading exercises

2	(a)	*uult*	Where does the poor man want to have a huge dinner?
	(b)	*uis*	Where do you wish to enter?
	(c)	*uult*	Every poor man wishes to bear the worries of a rich man.
	(d)	*uolumus*	We slaves wish to love beautiful girls and to carry off our master's gold.
	(e)	*uolunt*	All citizens want to bear an easy burden.
	(f)	*uultis*	You never wish to cook dinner at Euclio's house.

pp.74–5 Reading exercise/Test exercise

Megadorus wants to hold marriage-rites. He therefore summons many cooks to the house. The task of the cooks is to cook a huge dinner. Megadorus is bringing home as his wife Phaedra, the daughter of Euclio. But the cooks consider Euclio a poor man and a gloomy one. For he wants to lose nothing. When he wishes to sleep, he places a huge bag over his mouth. In this way, he doesn't lose breath while he is sleeping. At the barber's because he wants to lose nothing, he collects all the nail-clippings and takes them home. He's not willing to give water. He's not willing to give fire, because he's afraid to lose (it). He's a gloomy man. Therefore the cooks want to enter the house of Megadorus, a rich and easy man. But there is much danger in Megadorus' house, huge silver pots, many clothes, much gold. If the slaves lose anything, they think the cooks (are) thieves and want to seize (them). But at Euclio's house cooks are safe. It is not easy to carry off silver pots from Euclio's house, because he has no pots!

English–Latin

(a) Why do you (pl.) want to carry a load into the house of Megadorus, a rich man?
cenamne in aedibus Euclionis, uiri pauperis, coquere uultis?

(b) Every citizen wants (*or* all the citizens want) to get out of danger.
serui audaces fugere ex aedibus uolunt.

(c) Who wants to lose a huge (sum of) money?
quae femina seruum audacem inuenire non uult?

(d) When rich men hold marriage-rites, they summon cooks into the house.
domini ubi cenam magnam uolunt, coquum bonum rogant.

(e) All cooks carry huge knives.
femina pulchra turbam magnam fert.

(f) However at a poor man's house dinner is gloomy.
apud diuitem cenae optimae sunt.

Section 1G

pp.79–80 Exercises

1 *seni misero*
senibus miseris
puellae audaci
puellis audacibus
puero ingenti
pueris ingentibus
oneri multo
oneribus multis
consilio audaci
consiliis audacibus

2 *animo, uirtuti, audaciae, diuitibus, oneri, filiis, aquae, domino, ignibus, dis, feminis, coronae, consilio*

3 *seruis ingentibus*
mihi
seni misero
uxoribus malis
nobis, tibi

4 (a) Then the Lar of the household gives Euclio a pot full of gold.
(b) The wretched old man however entrusts all the gold to the shrine.
(c) But the bold slave wants to take the gold away from the wretched old man.
(d) However, Euclio shouts in this way to the wicked slave: 'What business have you got in the shrine? What are you taking away from me?'
(e) Therefore the slave is afraid and doesn't take away the gold from Euclio.
(f) But Euclio takes away the pot from out of the shrine, because now he doesn't want to entrust the gold to the god.

pp.80–81 Exercises

2 *cura, animo, audaciis, homine, uxore, pecunia, filiis, domino, ignibus, honoribus, femina, coronis, consilio, scelere*

3 *in fano*
a femina
ex aquis
in scelere
ex animo
in consiliis
ex ignibus

4 (a) Euclio is a man of the utmost self-control.
(b) Lyconides is a young man of the greatest beauty, but of no self-control.
(c) Be of a calm frame of mind, my son.
(d) You are a slave-woman of the greatest boldness and the greatest beauty, but of no self-control.
(e) I am in a cheerful frame of mind, because I consider my daughter (to be) a girl of the greatest goodness.

5 (a) Fortune helps the brave.
(b) No one is faithful in love.
(c) All art is an imitation of nature.
(d) Truth lies open for everyone.
(e) Death is common to every age.
(f) The gods care for great things, but do not bother with small ones.
(g) The British have long hair, and have every part of their body shaved except their head and upper lip.

pp.81–2 Reading exercises

1 (a) The bold slave says many wicked things to the wretched old man.
(b) Show me ointment (and) garlands and gold.
(c) There is too much worry for my wife at home.
(d) Why do you not give back my gold to me?

(e) I promise my daughter to you because you are a good neighbour.
(f) Beautiful wives always take away gold from rich men, because they want to give much money to the cooks.
(g) I give you many slaves and much money.
(h) I never entrust anything to a bold slave and a beautiful slave-woman.
(i) I wish to promise my daughter to a rich man, because I have no dowry.
(j) We have a garland at home, you (pl.) have ointment.

2 *(possible answers)*

(a)	*dant*	All citizens give money to good men.
(b)	*das*	Why do you give me gold?
(c)	*est*	We are in a cheerful frame of mind.
(d)	*credit*	Euclio entrusts the gold to the shrine, not to the bold man.
(e)	*aufers*	Why do you take away all the garlands and all the ointment from us?
(f)	*est*	Bold girls and handsome young men have no self-control.
(g)	*celo*	I hide from the man my daughter's dowry.
(h)	*promittit*	Why does your father not promise you as a wife to me?
(i)	*est*	You villain, what business do you have in my house?
(j)	*dat*	Boldness gives courage to every good young man.

p.82 Reading exercise/Test exercise

Euclio has a pot full of gold. Euclio carries the pot out of the house. For he is very afraid. For thieves always want to take all the gold away from every good man. Therefore he wants to hide the pot in the shrine. When Euclio hides the gold in the shrine, Strobilus sees. Euclio leaves the shrine. He is in a cheerful frame of mind, because he now fears no thief. Strobilus however creeps like a worm into the shrine. For he wishes to carry the pot off from the wretched Euclio. But Euclio sees the bold slave. He says many bad things to the bold slave, and demands his gold. But the slave doesn't want to give back the gold to the old man, because he doesn't have the gold. The slave shows his right hand to Euclio. Then he shows his left hand to the wretched old man. However Euclio asks for his third hand. The slave considers Euclio mad, and goes out. Euclio carries the pot out of the shrine and entrusts it secretly to another place.

p.83 English–Latin

(a) Euclio is a man of the greatest goodness.
Phaedra puella summa pulchritudine est.

(b) Be cheerful and give me the money.
aequo animo es et aurum seruo aufer.

(c) The wretched old man entrusts the pot full of gold to a wicked man.
omnes senes ciuibus bonis aulas pecuniae plenas reddunt.

(d) But why do you not give back the gold to the old man?
uos autem quare coronam iuueni aufertis?

(e) What business have you (s.) in the house of the wretched old man?
quid uobis negoti est in fano Laris mei?

(f) I've an excellent father, a man of the greatest self-control.
est mihi filius optimus, iuuenis summis uirtutibus.

Section Two

Section 2A

p.89 Exercises

1	*celabunt*	they will hide	*celabit*	1
	inueniet	he will find	*inuenient*	4
	amittes	you (s.) will lose	*amittetis*	3
	habebimus	we shall have	*habebo*	2
	coquent	they will cook	*coquet*	3
	iubebit	he will order	*iubebunt*	2
	uerberabis	you (s.) will beat	*uerberabitis*	1
	credet	he will believe	*credent*	3
	capietis	you (pl.) will capture	*capies*	3/4
	scribam	I shall write	*scribemus*	3
	facient	they will do	*faciet*	3/4
	audietis	you (pl.) will hear	*audies*	4

2	*credunt*	*credent*	they will believe
	salutat	*salutabit*	he will greet
	scribit	*scribet*	he will write
	fers	*feres*	you (s.) will bear
	estis	*eritis*	you (pl.) will be
	it	*ibit*	he will go
	rogo	*rogabo*	I shall ask
	curant	*curabunt*	they will take care of

3	*do*	*dabit*	he will give
		dabunt	they will give
	clamo	*clamabit*	he will shout
		clamabunt	they will shout
	maneo	*manebit*	he will wait
		manebunt	they will wait
	taceo	*tacebit*	he will be silent
		tacebunt	they will be silent
	duco	*ducet*	he will lead
		ducent	they will lead
	posco	*poscet*	he will demand
		poscent	they will demand
	dormio	*dormiet*	he will sleep
		dormient	they will sleep
	uincio	*uinciet*	he will bind
		uincient	they will bind
	capio	*capiet*	he will capture
		capient	they will capture
	fugio	*fugiet*	he will flee
		fugient	they will flee
	sum	*erit*	he will be
		erunt	they will be
	redeo	*redibit*	he will return
		redibunt	they will return

4	you (s.) will hear	*audies*
	they will call	*uocabunt*
	I shall make	*faciam*
	we will speak	*dicemus*
	you (pl.) will be silent	*tacebitis*
	he will lead	*ducet*
	we will love	*amabimus*

5	*ducent*	they will lead
	uerberabo	I shall beat
	duces	you (s.) will lead
	amabunt	they will like

fugiemus	we shall flee
mittes	you (s.) will send
decipies	you (s.) will deceive

All other verbs in this exercise are in the present tense.

If you have got the wrong answer in any of these exercises, check that you have identified the conjugation of the verb correctly, and check whether the verb is irregular.

p.90 Exercises

1	you (s.) wish	*uis*
	we prefer	*malumus*
	they refuse	*nolunt*
	he can	*potest*
	we will prefer	*malemus*
	you (pl.) do not wish	*non uultis*
	you (s.) are able	*potes*
	they will refuse	*nolent*

2	*est*	he is	*erit*	he will be
	possunt	they can	*poterunt*	they will be able
	uoles	you (s.) will wish	*uis*	you wish
	malent	they will prefer	*malunt*	they prefer
	non uis	you (s.) do not wish	*noles*	you (s.) will not wish
	erimus	we shall be	*sumus*	we are
	nolumus	we do not want	*nolemus*	we shall not want

p.93 Exercises

1	beautiful hand	*manus pulchra*
	large hand	*manus magna*
	my hand	*manus mea*
	swift hand	*manus celeris*

N.B. *manus – us* (4) is a feminine noun.

2	*uia*	ablative sing. (without macron = nominative)
	amicae	dative sing. (*or* genitive sing. *or* nominative pl.)

nocte	ablative sing.
manui	dative sing.
celeri	dative *or* ablative sing.
officio facili	dative *or* ablative sing.
scelere audaci	ablative sing.
soli	dative sing.
nummis ducentis	dative *or* ablative pl.
astutiae tuae	dative sing. *or* genitive sing. *or* nominative pl.
sumptui magno	dative sing.

If you have made any mistakes, check the declension of the nouns and adjectives.

p.94 Exercises

1 (a) Today our old man will give you two hundred coins into the hand.

(b) What do you want me to do? For I prefer to help rather than to do nothing.

(c) If the old man considers me a liar, I shall want to play many tricks.

(d) I shall do my duty; I prefer you to do yours.

(e) If I can remove the gold (away) from the old man, you will be able to give two hundred coins to your friends.

(f) Give me your hand, I beg you; I shall give you mine.

(g) If you are willing to trust a woman, you are willing to write in running water.

(h) If you can get the gold away from the old man, Chrysalus, I shall consider you a slave of great astuteness.

(i) While the night is silent, thieves prefer to commit wicked crimes (rather) than to sleep.

(j) Take the wax, tablets and pen away from me; today I do not wish to write.

2 (a) Experience is the best teacher.

(b) But who will guard the guards themselves?

(c) The deeds of mortals never fool the gods.

(d) It is rage that helps lions, fear stags, vehemence the hawk and flight the dove.
(e) Just as a great man can emerge from a hovel, so a beautiful and mighty soul can emerge from an ugly and lowly little body.
(f) No man can be happy without virtue.
(g) Without control neither house nor state can survive.

pp.96–7 Reading exercise/Test exercise

Here is Chrysalus, the bold slave of Nicobulus, a man of great talent and the utmost astuteness. Through Chrysalus, Mnesilochus wants to deceive the old man a second time. Chrysalus has a difficult job. The old man trusts neither Chrysalus nor his son. But Chrysalus adopts a bold plan. He sends Pistoclerus, Mnesilochus' friend, into the house. He orders Pistoclerus to bring wax, tablets, pen and thread. When the friend returns, Chrysalus orders Mnesilochus to write a letter to his father. The good son writes to his father in this way: 'Chrysalus is wicked, my (dear) father. For today he will come to you and he will aim a great catapult at you. For he considers you a town, old and full of gold. If he destroys your tower and your ramparts, he will immediately assault you (coming) through the gate into the town. Then he will order me to take away your gold from the town in baskets and give it to my mistress. I am telling you to be careful, my (dear) father. For the cost will be great, if he deceives you a second time. Farewell.'

p.97 English–Latin

(a) I order you to take my daughter home at once.
Mnesilochus Chrysalum senem miserum iterum decipere uolet.
(b) I always prefer the virtue of a poor man to the boldness of a rich man.
audacis serui astutias quam mendacis amicae audaciam semper malet.
(c) Nicobulus, a man of no astuteness, will never be able to remove the gold from the bold slave.
Chrysalus, uir magna astutia, ducentos nummos seni facile auferre poterit.
(d) The cost of a mistress is always great.
furis manus semper celeris est.
(e) The rich give no coins to the poor.
senes iuuenibus pecuniam dabunt multam.
(f) I shall have a lot of expense because I have a rich wife.
erunt iuuenibus magni sumptus, quod amicas habent pulchras.

Section 2B

p.104 Exercises

For this exercise *-re* endings have been treated as indicative, though of course they could also be imperative singular.

1

precatur	he prays	*precantur*	they pray
mentiris	you (s.) lie	*mentimini*	you (pl.) lie
pollicemur	we promise	*polliceor*	I promise
sequuntur	they follow	*sequitur*	he follows
minaris	you (s.) threaten	*minamini*	you (pl.) threaten
loquimini	you (pl.) speak	*loqueris*	you (s.) speak
mentior	I lie	*mentimur*	we lie
opinare	you think (s.)	*opinamini*	you think (pl.)
progredimini	you (pl.) advance	*progrederis*	you (s.) advance
loqueris	you (s.) speak	*loquimini*	you (pl.) speak
pollicere	you promise (s.)	*pollicemini*	you promise (pl.)
minamur	we threaten	*minor*	I threaten

2

we threaten	*minamur*
he promises	*pollicetur*
they forget	*obliuiscuntur*
you (pl.) remember	*recordamini*
you (s.) speak	*loqueris*
I am following	*sequor*
advance! (s.)	*progredere*
beg! (s.)	*precare*
talk! (pl.)	*loquimini!*
promise! (s.)	*pollicere!*

3

Infinitives		**Imperatives**	
amare	to love	*minare*	threaten! (s.)
uocare	to call	*pollicere*	promise! (s.)
habere	to have	*sequere*	follow! (s.)
loqui	to speak	*audi*	listen! (s.)
inuenire	to find	*dormi*	sleep! (s.)
progredi	to advance	*precare*	pray! (s.)

mentiri	to lie	*inueni*	find! (s.)
opinari	to think	*loquere*	speak! (s.)
ducere	to lead	*progredere*	advance! (s.)
inire	to go in		
iubere	to order		

4	*habeo*	I have	*habere*	*habe!*
	curo	I care for	*curare*	*cura!*
	minor	I threaten	*minari*	*minare!*
	loquor	I speak	*loqui*	*loquere!*
	audio	I hear	*audire*	*audi!*
	duco	I lead	*ducere*	*duc! (irregular)*
	mitto	I send	*mittere*	*mitte!*
	precor	I pray	*precari*	*precare!*
	fugio	I flee	*fugere*	*fuge!*
	credo	I trust	*credere*	*crede!*

p.105 Exercise

don't (s.) follow	*noli sequi*
don't (pl.) threaten me	*nolite mihi minari*
don't (s.) be stupid (m.)	*noli stultus esse*
don't (pl.) send the letter	*nolite litteras mittere*
don't (s.) hide the pot	*noli aulam celare*
don't (pl.) lead the slaves	*nolite seruos ducere*

p.105 Exercise

s.	**pl.**
omnis res	*omnes res*
omnem rem	*omnis (-es) res*
omnis rei	*omnium rerum*
omni rei	*omnibus rebus*
omni re	*omnibus rebus*

s.	**pl.**
pulcher dies	*pulchri dies*
pulchrum diem	*pulchros dies*
pulchri diei	*pulchrorum dierum*
pulchro diei	*pulchris diebus*
pulchro die	*pulchris diebus*
mea res	*meae res*
meam rem	*meas res*
meae rei	*mearum rerum*
meae rei	*meis rebus*
mea re	*meis rebus*
tristis dies	*tristes dies*
tristem diem	*tristis (-es) dies*
tristis diei	*tristium dierum*
tristi diei	*tristibus diebus*
tristi die	*tristibus diebus*

pp.106–7 Exercises

1 (a) Nicobulus: Don't threaten me, Chrysalus.
Chrysalus: But master, I'm telling you how it is. (*Literally,* So I am telling you as the thing is.)

(b) The bold slave has a head full of tricks.

(c) The slaves soon leave the house and follow the old man.

(d) But who is speaking? It's Chrysalus, I think. (*Literally,* As I think, it's Chrysalus.)

(e) Look inside, my (dear) master. What do you see in the house? It's a bad thing I think.

(f) *Literally,* Chrysalus tells his master to take care and calls him ignorant of all things.

(g) Find out everything. I prefer you to remember (rather) than to forget.

(h) As you promise, so I want it (the thing) to be.

(i) What do you think? Look! The slaves threatens me, next he lies, then he begs and beseeches me.

(j) Advance, my (dear) Nicobulus, and threaten Chrysalus at once.

2 (a) Love is (an) unsuspecting (thing).
(b) It is a great thing to be quiet.
(c) There will be crimes as long as there are men.
(d) Human affairs are frail and perishable.
(e) It is sweet and honourable to die for one's country.
(f) It is Roman both to do and to suffer brave deeds.

p.107 Reading

Literal translation only.

(a) Then you will find out everything, my (dear) master, if you want to know, when you see your son in the house of the Bacchides. (N.B. all the tenses in the Latin in this sentence are *future*, but need not be translated as such.)
(b) As you say the thing to me, so I think, because I trust you.
(c) Our old man is worth as much as a stinking mushroom, as Chrysalus thinks, because he is a slave of the utmost boldness.
(d) Because I want you to know everything, I will order you to look inside the house, where, if you have eyes, you will soon see your son with his girl friend.
(e) But if I can (shall be able to) give the old man the letter at the time when I want to, he will be as roasted as a roasted chick pea, as I think.

p.108 Reading exercise/Test exercise

Chrysalus pursues a mad business in his opinion (*literally*, as he thinks) because he wants to deceive the old man a second time. Yet the plan (he has) in mind is daring enough. For he will give the old man Mnesilochus' letter. Chrysalus wants his master to be mad at the time (*tum*) when he receives (*literally*, will receive) the letter, because then he will be able to tell of Mnesilochus' bad character. The bold slave gives the letter into the hands of the old man (*literally*, *to* the old man – *dative*) at the time when he is coming out of the house. The old man reads the letter, next he calls his slaves. Then, when they are leaving the house, he orders the slaves to tie up Chrysalus and (orders) Chrysalus to be quiet. But Chrysalus laughs at the old man and says he is (*literally*, calls him) ignorant of everything (of all things) and stupid. He considers his master, as he says, (to be) worth as much as a stinking mushroom. The old man becomes as angry as his slave wants. But then Chrysalus speaks of the danger of Mnesilochus (and) tells the old man to look inside the house of the Bacchides. The old man goes (*literally*, advances) to the house and looks inside. But he sees a dinner-party and a bad, sad affair.

p.108 English–Latin

(a) Don't approach my wife, Chrysalus.
noli seni misero (dative) *minari, serue.*

(b) When you write a letter, have the matter in mind; words soon follow.
ubi rem recordamini, pericula recordamini (or preferably *in animo habete*); *animus numquam mentitur.*
N.B. *recordor* = recall *and* remember

(c) (But) the rich man, ignorant of virtue, threatens the poor man.
serui autem, omnium rerum nescii, periculi (genitive) *obliuiscuntur.*

(d) The good citizens are going (*literally*, advancing) into danger.
puellae omnes ex aedibus egrediuntur.

(e) I am not threatening you, but I am saying how the matter stands (*literally*, how the thing is).
nos non mentimur, sed ita tibi (or *uobis*) *loquimur ut res est.*

(f) Follow me, my slaves, and forget everything.
sequere me in aedis, mi fili, et deos precare.

Section 2C

pp.115–6 Exercises

1

s.	pl.
hic seruus	*hi serui*
hunc seruum	*hos seruos*
huius serui	*horum seruorum*
huic seruo	*his seruis*
hoc seruo	*his seruis*
ille miles	*illi milites*
illum militem	*illos milites*
illius militis	*illorum militum*
illi militi	*illis militibus*
illo milite	*illis militibus*
haec serua	*hae seruae*
hanc seruam	*has seruas*
huius seruae	*harum seruarum*
huic seruae	*his seruis*
hac serua	*his seruis*
illud periculum	*illa pericula*
illud periculum	*illa pericula*
illius periculi	*illorum periculorum*
illi periculo	*illis periculis*
illo periculo	*illis periculis*
hoc uerbum	*haec uerba*
hoc uerbum	*haec uerba*
huius uerbi	*horum uerborum*
huic uerbo	*his uerbis*
hoc uerbo	*his uerbis*
illa mulier	*illae mulieres*
illam mulierem	*illas mulieres*
illius mulieris	*illarum mulierum*
illi mulieri	*illis mulieribus*
illa muliere	*illis mulieribus*

2 genitive; ablative; nominative; dative; nominative *or* accusative; dative *or* ablative

3 *hunc militem; illi seni; huius puellae; illa consilia; haec pericula; illius feminae*

4

4	*hi thesauri*	nom. pl.	*illas mulieres*	acc. pl.
	illius thesauri	gen. sing.	*hae mulieres*	nom. pl.
	illas sorores	acc. pl.	*illi puero*	dat. sing.
	hae sorores	nom. pl.	*hoc puero*	abl. sing.
	illa res	nom. sing.	*illae feminae*	nom. pl.
	has res	acc. pl.	*huic feminae*	dat. sing.
	illae res	nom. pl.	*illius feminae*	gen. sing.
	huius manus	gen. sing.	*hic dies*	nom. sing.
	illae manus	nom. pl.	*illos dies*	acc. pl.
	hae manus	nom. pl.	*hi dies*	nom. pl.

5	*huius amici*	this friend's	*gen. sing. masc./fem./neut.*
	huius lunae	this moon's	
	illum puerum	that boy	*acc. sing. masc.*
	illum fratrem	that brother	
	illa uxore	(by) that wife	*abl. sing. fem.*
	illa manu	by that hand	
	hoc officium	this duty	*nom./acc. sing. neut.*
	hoc aurum	this gold	
	hoc nomen	this name	
	haec corona	this crown	*nom. sing. fem.* (or *nom./acc.*
	haec negotia	these duties	*pl. neut.)*
	haec res	this thing	
	haec opera	these works	
	haec manus	this hand	
	illos ciuis	those citizens	*acc. pl. masc.*
	illos deos	those gods	

p.115 Optional revision

1

hide	1	*celare*
tell	1	*explicare*
find	4	*inuenire*
hear	4	*audire*
lead	3	*ducere*
flee	3/4	*fugere*
send	3	*mittere*
bear	irreg.	*ferre*
prefer	irreg.	*malle*
be	irreg.	*esse*
believe	3	*credere*
write	3	*scribere*
greet	1	*salutare*
read	3	*legere*
not to know	4	*nescire*

2

amabis	you will love	2nd person singular future active	*amo*
habere	to have	infinitive active	*habeo*
duc	lead!	imperative singular active	*duco*
minari	to threaten	infinitive deponent	*minor*
dicet	he will say	3rd person singular future active	*dico*
uelle	to want	infinitive active	*uolo*
scribitis	you write	2nd person plural present active	*scribo*
potero	I shall be able	1st person singular future active	*possum*
cape	take!	imperative singular active	*capio*
dormiunt	they sleep	3rd person plural present active	*dormio*
progredere	advance!	imperative singular deponent	*progredior*

defendis	you defend	2nd person singular present active	*defendo*
opprimes	you will surprise	2nd person singular future active	*opprimo*
neca	kill!	imperative singular active	*neco*
loqui	to speak	infinitive deponent	*loquor*
nolumus	we refuse	1st person plural present active	*nolo*
irridere	to laugh at	infinitive active	*irrideo*
state	stand!	imperative plural active	*sto*
rogas	you ask	2nd person singular present active	*rogo*

pp.116–8 Exercises

1 with these women
on that head
to this thing
through that crowd
with this prostitute
from that danger

2 *in hanc scaenam*
cum illa muliere
per hosignes
cum illis fratribus
in hoc oculo
in illud oppidum
per haec pericula

3 (a) If that solider catches Mnesilochus with Bacchis, he will kill them.
(b) This Bacchis seems to be the girlfriend of Mnesilochus, that one of Pistoclerus.
(c) That young man loves this woman, and this one loves that one.
(d) Nicobulus hears the words of that soldier, then he clearly gets to know the character of his son.

(e) All prostitutes seem evil to this slave and excellent to those young men.

(f) That slave tries to deceive this old man.

4 (a) The one salvation for the conquered is to hope for no salvation.

(b) We cannot change the past.

(c) We always strive towards the forbidden and yearn for what we have been denied.

(d) Once spoken the word flies beyond recall.

pp.116–7 Reading

(a) That soldier (subject) this woman (object) to/for this young man (dative) to believe.
ille miles hanc mulierem huic iuueni credere uult.
That soldier wants this woman to believe this young man.

(b) that slaves (object) of this old man.
illum huius senis seruum uideo.
I see that slave of this old man.

(c) this gold (object) to/for that soldier this slave (subject).
hoc aurum illi militi hic seruus dat.
this slave gives this gold to that soldier.

(d) with this woman that young man (object) this soldier (subject) soon.
cum hac muliere illum iuuenem hic miles mox uidebit.
This soldier will soon see that young man with this woman.

(e) to this woman he (subject) all these coins (object) to give.
huic ille feminae hos nummos omnis dare mauult.
He prefers to give all these coins to this woman.

p.117 Reading exercise/Test exercise

A literal analysis:

Nicobulus (subject) his son and Bacchis (object) in the house sees (*uidet*). The prostitute (subject) Bacchis (subject) is (*est*). To/for Chrysalus however a prostitute (subject) to be she (*illa*) does not seem. Now enters Cleomachus the soldier (subject) and of that prostitute (*meretricis*) the lover. Him (object) however Chrysalus (subject) of Bacchis the husband (*uirum*) calls. Of Chrysalus the master (subject) now fears greatly (*ualde*), because Bacchis (object) of the soldier wife (object) s/he thinks. Of Chrysalus the hands (object, subject *or* gen.) the slaves (object) immediately to release (*exsoluere*) he orders, Chrysalus (object) with this soldier (*milite*) to make a bargain, what he wants. To this soldier the slave (subject) immediately coins (object) many (*multos*) promises. But him (object) to be silent and evil words (subject) to hear (*audire*) he orders, because the old man (object) to deceive (*decipere*) he wants. Then the coins (object) to the soldier he (*ille*) promises, Chrysalus (subject) however to that soldier many false things he says about Mnesilochus (*de Mnesilocho*) and him (object) to the forum sends.

A more English version:

Nicobulus sees his son and Bacchis in the house. Bacchis is a prostitute. To Chrysalus however, she doesn't seem to be a prostitute. Now Cleomachus the soldier – that prostitute's lover – enters. Chrysalus however calls him the husband of Bacchis. The master of Chrysalus now fears greatly, because he thinks Bacchis is the wife of the soldier. He immediately orders the slaves to untie the hands of Chrysalus, and Chrysalus to make the bargain with this soldier which he wants. To this soldier the slave immediately promises many coins. But he orders him to be silent and to hear some bad words because he wants to deceive the old man. Then he promises the soldier the coins. Chrysalus however utters many insults to that soldier about Mnesilochus and sends him to the forum.

pp.117–8 English–Latin

1 (a) *illius filiam hic amat.*
(b) *pater huius iuuenis diues esse uidetur.*
(c) *illas meretrices arbitror.*
(d) *hoc bonis ciuibus magnum officium est.*
(e) *ille miles hanc mulierem defendere uult.*
(f) *mores harum malos arbitror.*

2 CHR. *quis est hic homo?*
NIC. *est filius meus Mnesilochus.*
CHR. *bella cum muliere esse uidetur. quid opinaris?*
NIC. *bella est, sed quis est? dic mihi, precor.*
CHR. *illumne uides?*

NIC. *militemne illum dicis?*

CHR. *ita.*

NIC. *age nunc.*

CHR. *ita faciam. huius mulieris uir est.*

NIC. *quid dicis? sed haec mulier plane meretrix est.*

CHR. *hocne arbitraris? scies mox omnia.*

NIC. *quid? nuptane est illa? perii. me miserum! scelestum iuuenem!*

Section 2D

p.126 Exercises

All these verbs follow the patterns set out on p.122.

1	*clamo*	*clamaui*
		clamauisti etc.
	uideo	*uidi*
		uidisti etc.
	uinco	*uici*
		uicisti etc.
	uincio	*uinxi*
		uinxisti etc.
	abeo	*abiui* (or *abii*)
		abiuisti (or *abiisti*) etc.
	sum	*fui*
		fuisti etc.
	do	*dedi*
		dedisti etc.
	capio	*cepi*
		cepisti etc.
	fero	*tuli*
		tulisti etc.
	facio	*feci*
		fecisti etc.

If you made a mistake in forming these perfects, check the perfect stems on pp.123–6.

2	*deleuisti*	you (s.) destroyed	*deleuistis*
	gesserunt	they did, acted	*gessit*
	uicit	he conquered	*uicerunt*
	adfuistis	you (pl.) were present	*adfuisti*
	solui	I released	*soluimus*
	pugnauimus	we fought	*pugnaui*
	abiistis	you (pl.) went away	*abiisti*

3	*do*	you (s.) gave
	credo	he believed
	adfero	they brought
	sum	he was
	debeo	you (pl.) owed (ought)
	maneo	I remained
	opprimo	we surprised (etc.)
	scribo	they wrote
	adiuuo	you (pl.) helped
	tango	he touched
	amitto	you (s.) lost
	dico	we said
	exeo	he went out

4 *dedi; pugnauimus; deleuisti; amauit; adfuerunt; uicistis; exii; necauerunt; respondit; gessisti; perfecimus; tulistis*

5	**pres.**	**fut.**	**perf.**
s.	*dormit*	*dormiet*	*dormiuit*
pl.	*dormiunt*	*dormient*	*dormiuerunt*
s.	*pugnat*	*pugnabit*	*pugnauit*
pl.	*pugnant*	*pugnabunt*	*pugnauerunt*
s.	*delet*	*delebit*	*deleuit*
pl.	*delent*	*delebunt*	*deleuerunt*
s.	*gerit*	*geret*	*gessit*
pl.	*gerunt*	*gerent*	*gesserunt*
s.	*est*	*erit*	*fuit*
pl.	*sunt*	*erunt*	*fuerunt*
s.	*aufert*	*auferet*	*abstulit*
pl.	*auferunt*	*auferent*	*abstulerunt*
s.	*redit*	*redibit*	*rediit*
pl.	*redeunt*	*redibunt*	*redierunt*
s.	*decipit*	*decipiet*	*decepit*
pl.	*decipiunt*	*decipient*	*deceperunt*

6	*stabit*	future
	dederunt	they gave
	credet	future
	aderis	future
	uicisti	you conquered
	pugnabunt	future
	soluunt	present
	delent	present
	gerent	future
	mansi	I remained
	inuenistis	you found
	perficies	future
	diligis	present
	habes	present
	monuistis	you warned

p.127 Exercise

1 (a) Mnesilochus silently listened to the words of Chrysalus.
(b) I fought with a soldier, presently I shall fight with an old man, now however I am silent.
(c) A long time afterwards the Greeks captured the city of Troy.
(d) At this time of night everyone ought to be asleep.
(e) Silently thieves enter the house secretly by night.
(f) As the Greeks sent the horse against Troy at that time, so today Chrysalus will send writing tablets against his master.

2 (a) The defender of a fault says to me, 'We also did this as young men'.
(b) Tell me, what have I done, except that I have not loved wisely?
(c) We were Trojans: Troy was (Troy has existed, is a 'has been').
(d) You have played enough, eaten and drunk enough; it is time for you to leave.
(e) Nature has given us the seeds for knowledge; it has not given knowledge.

pp.127–8 Reading exercise

a very bold man (a); at that time (c); on this night (c); about your danger (b); in the silent night (c); by sad old men (b); a very astute slave (a); with me (b); in many hours (c); a long time afterwards (c); a very beautiful woman (a); out of the forum (b); at that time of night (c); with my wife (b); in ten years (c)

p.128 Reading exercise/Test exercise

The sons of Atreus a long time afterwards captured Ilium. For in the tenth year they at last stormed the city of Troy. For at the time the kings sent a wooden horse into the city. Epeus, a very astute man, built that horse. Armed soldiers were in the horse, very bold men. These men came out of the horse that night and soon destroyed the city. Thus on that day the city of Troy perished in one hour.

pp.128–9 English–Latin

1 (a) *iuuenis in aedibus stetit tacitus.*
(b) *senexne aurum militi dedit?*
(c) *equos contra urbem Troiam miserunt.*
(d) *hac nocte meum dominum uici et multam praedam cepi.*
(e) *hoc anni tempore omnes domi manere debent.*
(f) *milites signum uiderunt et mox contra oppidum progredientur.*

2 NIC. *quid facere debeo, Chrysale? dic mihi.*
CHR. *nolo.*
NIC. *dic, quaeso. quid faciam? nam rem bene gerere uolo.*
CHR. *rem bene geres, ut ego opinor, si aurum filio tuo dabis. sed ego non iubeo.*
NIC. *nummos ei dabo. mane hic! mox huc reueniam. (Nicobulus in aedis intrat)*
CHR. *adest exitium senis! ut eum decepi! nunc Mnesilochus amicae satis nummorum dare poterit.*

Section 2E

pp.135–6 Exercises

1	*opinabor*	*opinabimur*
	opinaberis	*opinabimini*
	opinabitur	*opinabuntur*
	conspicabor	*conspicabimur*
	conspicaberis	*conspicabimini*
	conspicabitur	*conspicabuntur*
	uidebor	*uidebimur*
	uideberis	*uidebimini*
	uidebitur	*uidebuntur*
	irascar	*irascemur*
	irasceris	*irascemini*
	irascetur	*irascentur*
	obliuiscar	*obliuiscemur*
	obliuisceris	*obliuiscemini*
	obliuiscetur	*obliuiscentur*
	mentiar	*mentiemur*
	mentieris	*mentiemini*
	mentietur	*mentientur*
	egrediar	*egrediemur*
	egredieris	*egrediemini*
	egredietur	*egredientur*
	patiar	*patiemur*
	patieris	*patiemini*
	patietur	*patientur*
2	I shall think	*opinabimur*
	you will lie	*mentiemini*
	he/she will pray	*precabuntur*
	you will seem	*uideberis* (or *uidebere)*
	you will speak	*loquemini*
	we shall promise	*pollicebor*

3 *precaberis; minabitur; uidebuntur; loquemini; progrediar; opinabimur; conabuntur; sequetur*

4

minabitur	he/she will threaten
precabuntur	they will pray
opinabor	I shall think
uidebimini	you will seem
conspicabitur	he/she will catch sight of
sequetur	he/she will follow
loquentur	they will speak

5

arbitraris	you think
conatur	he/she tries
patiuntur	they suffer
loquimini	you speak
sequimur	we follow
adgrederis	you go up to
moror	I delay
opinamur	we think
progredimini	you advance
uidetur	he/she seems
mentior	I am lying

6

dedit	he gave	perfect
conaberis	you will try	future
mentitur	he lies	present
uidebitur	he will seem	future
fecerunt	they made	perfect
amant	they like	present
delent	they destroy	present
dicent	they will say	future
loqueris	you (s.) will speak	future
tulisti	you (s.) have carried	perfect

pp.136–7 Exercises

1 (a) Nicobulus called his son a worthless young man.
(b) Philoxenus, however, considered mistresses nothing but good.
(c) Nicobulus is threatening Bacchis with death if she will not release his son.
(d) Because he is in love, Philoxenus seems to Nicobulus to be as valuable as a rotten mushroom.
(e) Bacchis! I order you to embrace that old man. I shall embrace this one (note the mistake in *GVE* – *amplexor* is first conjugation and the future should be *amplexabor*).
(f) Sister! I shall deal with the old man as you ordered, although it seems to me a great evil to embrace death.
(g) In my opinion, both old men will soon advance to the doors.
(h) It is just as I said. The old men are advancing to the doors.

2 (a) The humble have a hard time when the powerful disagree.
(b) Divine nature gave the fields, human skill built the cities.
(c) For I remember, I remember and I shall never forget that night.
(d) Here, where Rome, the capital of the world, now is, was a tree, grass, a few cattle and the odd cottage.
(e) Religion has produced wicked and impious deeds.
(f) Nobody is ever an utter scoundrel suddenly.

pp.137–8 Reading and Reading exercise/Test exercise

1	(a)	+ *quod amator*	I consider you worthless, you rotten fellow, for this reason, because you dare to become a lover although you are an old man.
	(b)	+ *nisi bonum*	I consider life nothing if not a good thing.
	(c)	+ *quam uitam*	Old men always prefer death to life.
	(d)	+ *nisi nobis*	I shall give you great trouble, Bacchis, if you do not return our sons to us.
	(e)	+ *quamquam Mnesilochum*	Nicobulus however will receive gold and will enter the house of the Bacchises although he prefers to avenge Mnesilochus and Chrysalus.

(f)	+ *dum uiuis*	You must treat yourself well at this time while you live.
(g)	+ *ubi ad fores*	You will then catch sight of your son when you approach the doors of the Bacchises and look inside.

2 Philoxenus, father of Pistoclerus, a man of outstanding goodness, came on to the stage. There he saw Nicobulus, father of Mnesilochus. Nicobulus told Philoxenus many bad things about their sons. At length they approached the house of the Bacchises, they beat on the doors and called the prostitutes. Then when those women had come out of the house, they demanded their sons. At length the prostitutes took the old men into their house.

p.138 English–Latin

1 (a) *nisi pecuniam (meam) mihi reddes, te necabo.*

(b) *nihil nisi seruus mendax me sollicitat.*

(c) *ille senex tanti est quanti seruus scelestus.*

(d) *filium meum, si ad me adgredi audebit, amplexabor/complectar.*

(e) *illo tempore nullam uocem nisi tuam audire poteram.*

(f) *quamquam uita bonum est, mors ad ianuas et diuitum et pauperum adibit.*

Section Three

Section 3A

pp.144–5 Exercises

1

id bellum	*ea bella*	*bellum* is 2nd declension neuter
id bellum	*ea bella*	
eius belli	*eorum bellorum*	
ei bello	*eis bellis*	
eo bello	*eis bellis*	
ea urbs	*eae urbes*	*urbs* is 3rd declension feminine
eam urbem	*eas urbes*	
eius urbis	*earum urbium*	
ei urbi	*eis urbibus*	
ea urbe	*eis urbibus*	
is dux	*ei duces*	*dux* is 3rd declension masculine
eum ducem	*eos duces*	
eius ducis	*eorum ducum*	
ei duci	*eis ducibus*	
eo duce	*eis ducibus*	

2 gen. sing., nom. pl., dat. sing., dat./abl. pl., acc. sing., gen. pl., nom./acc. pl., nom. sing., acc. sing., acc. pl.

3 *(per) eos dies; eam uictoriam; eius belli; eis regibus; eos duces; id imperium; ei amicae; ei mores; eius; eis; eius; ei; ei; ea nocte*

4	*ei* is nom. pl. masc. *or* dat. sing. masc./fem./neut.	nom. pl. dat. sing.	*uiri, patres* *feminae, exercitui, puero*
	eae is nom. pl. fem.	nom. pl.	*amicae, res*
	ea is nom. fem. sing. *or* nom./acc. neut. pl.	nom. pl. nom. sing.	*imperia, capita* *astutia, uirtus, urbs, manus*
	eius is gen. sing. masc./fem./neut.	gen. sing.	*operis, pueri, rei, exercitus*
	eis is dat./abl. pl.		*signis, meretricibus, uiris, moribus*

5 in that town
because of that courage
at their house
at that time
along/through that road
with her
on that night
into that city
for those hours
towards those soldiers
through that night
for many days
in that year
that time

6 *cum eis feminis*
ea hora
apud eum
in eam scaenam
in eis urbibus
ob ea pericula
eis noctibus
propter id bellum
per eas horas

7 (a) *hae* These women are beautiful.
(b) *illos* Do you see those soldiers?
(c) *eius* It's enough of that war.
(d) *illius* That man's head is huge.
(e) *earum* A crowd of those women is coming in.

p.147 Exercise

diem longiorem, longissimum; nocte longiore, longissima; milites celeriores, celerrimi (-os); oculo celeriori or *oculo celeriore, celerrimo; aedes ingentiores, ingentissimae; familiam ingentiorem, ingentissimam; manus pulchrioris (-es),* or *manus pulcherrimas, pulcherrimae; mulierum pulchriorum, pulcherrimarum; consilia stultiora, stultissima; homini stultiori, stultissimo; operum stultiorum, stultissimorum.*

pp.148–9 Exercises

1

liber	free	*liberior*	freer	*liberrimus*	freest, most free, very free etc.
fortis	brave	*fortior*	braver	*fortissimus*	very brave etc.
bonus	good	*melior*	better	*optimus*	best
niger	black	*nigrior*	blacker	*nigerrimus*	blackest
similis	like	*similior*	more like	*simillimus*	most like
magnus	big	*maior*	bigger	*maximus*	biggest
celer	quick	*celerior*	quicker	*celerrimus*	quickest
paruus	small	*minor*	smaller	*minimus*	smallest
scelestus	wicked	*scelestior*	more wicked	*scelestissimus*	most wicked
stultus	stupid	*stultior*	more stupid	*stultissimus*	most stupid
malus	bad	*peior*	worse	*pessimus*	worst
tristis	sad	*tristior*	sadder	*tristissimus*	saddest
facilis	easy	*facilior*	easier	*facillimus*	easiest
multus	much	*plus*	more	*plurimus*	most
ingens	huge	*ingentior*	huger	*ingentissimus*	hugest

2 (a) For that night the king of gods and men stayed with that woman in the house.
(b) Her husband, Amphitruo, left home with a very strong army.
(c) She thinks Jupiter (is) Amphitruo because he made himself like Amphitruo.

(d) That god is loving her the whole night long because he has never seen a more beautiful woman than her.

(e) He made that night longer because of Alcumena.

(f) Or rather, he made that night the longest of all nights.

(g) Mercury, his son, is a god of the greatest cunning. In fact he is more cunning than all the gods and men.

(h) He made himself very like the slave Sosia.

(i) Amphitruo will return home this night because he has been successful in war and has carried off a very great victory.

(j) I have never seen a more stupid slave than Sosia, (or) a more wicked god than Mercury on the stage.

3 (a) Later thoughts, so they say, are usually wiser.

(b) Golden reins/a golden bridle doesn't make a horse better.

(c) I see better things and I approve of them, but I pursue worse things. (I realize the better way to act but I follow the worse way.)

(d) No slavery is more degrading than (a) voluntary (one). (*A premise of Stoic philosophy – free men could be dictated to by desire and physical passion.*)

(e) Love reason! Love of this will arm you against the most difficult situations/things.

p.149 Reading

(a)	*quam hanc*	I have never seen a longer night than this.
(b)	*quam ille*	This slave is bolder than that one.
(c)	*quam huic*	I shall give that old man more gold than this one.
(d)	*quam illo*	Night is blacker at this time than at that.
(e)	*quam hic*	That man is more courageous than this one.
(f)	*quam mendacem*	I prefer a very foolish slave to a deceitful one.
(g)	*quam hoc*	I shall never be able to bear greater danger than this.
(h)	*quam illi*	There were never braver soldiers than those.
(i)	*quam eum*	Have you ever seen a man more like a god than him?
(j)	*quam eas*	Shall I ever spot more beautiful women than those?

p.150 Reading exercise/Test exercise

Mercury, the craftiest of gods, comes to the city of Thebes with his father because he loves a very beautiful woman, the wife of the general of the Theban legions. Although that woman is married, Jupiter still wants to lie with her for the whole night. As we see, gods can be freer from these things (restrictions, scruples, problems) than men can, because they have very great power and never suffer death. However, Alcumena really loves her husband. Jupiter therefore brings Mercury with him because he knows the most/very many tricks and the best deceptions. Mercury therefore has made himself like Sosia, Amphitruo's slave, and Jupiter very like/the spitting image of Amphitruo. The gods have entered Amphitruo's house like this. Jupiter, king of gods and men, has loved Alcumena secretly all night long and has made her pregnant. In fact he has made her more pregnant, because Amphitruo also made her pregnant that night when he went off to war. Now the greatest god has made the night longer because he really loves Alcumena and has placed Mercury in front of the house. Soon Sosia will approach the house and try to enter, and Mercury will drive him away from the house.

pp.150–51 English–Latin

1 (a) *haec uictoria maior erat quam illa.*

(b) *illis annis, multi milites fortissimi, propter imperium regis stultioris, bellum longissimum gesserunt.*

(c) *nihil melius est quam officium ciuium optimorum.*

(d) *sapientia deorum maior est quam hominum.*

(e) *frater meus similior est patri/patris quam ego.*

(f) *nihil peius est quam hoc malum.*

2 SOS. *quis est melior quam ego?*

MERC. *quis turpior?*

SOS. *immo uero, ego optimus sum omnium seruorum, omnium hominum fortissimus.*

MERC. *et stultissimus stultorum.*

SOS. *audacior sum quia, hac nocte longissima, per has uias solus ambulo neque certe nigriorem nec longiorem noctem quam hanc umquam uidi. cur luna non se mutat neque haec signa occidunt? numquamne dies apparebit?*

MERC. *te, nox, ut nunc pergis, pergere uolo. numquam enim officium maius patri meo quam hoc exsequeris.*

Section 3B

pp.157–8 Exercises

2

locutus sum	I spoke	*locuti sumus*	we spoke
uisum est	it seemed	*uisa sunt*	they (n.) seemed
recordata est	she remembered	*recordatae sunt*	they (f.) remembered
mentiti sumus	we (m.) lied	*mentitus sum*	I (m.) lied
ingressae sunt	they (f.) entered	*ingressa est*	she entered
pollicita es	you (f.) promised	*pollicitae estis*	you (f.) promised
secuta sunt	they (n.) followed	*secutum est*	it followed
adeptus est	he got/obtained	*adepti sunt*	they (m.) got

3	*uideor*	he seemed
	adipiscor	she got
	obliuiscor	I forgot
	ingredior	we (women) entered
	loquor	you (pl.) spoke
	proficiscor	they set out
	fio (see p.157)	it became

4 *minata est*
profecti sunt
hortatus sum
uisa es
oblitae sumus
pollicitus est (*promisit* exists too)
factum est
mentiti estis

5	*irascitur*	he/she is angry
	irascuntur	they are angry
	irascetur	he/she will be angry
	irascentur	they will be angry
	iratus/a est	he/she was angry
	irati/ae sunt	they were angry

minatur	he/she threatens
minantur	they threaten
minabitur	he/she will threaten
minabuntur	they will threaten
minatus/a est	he/she threatened
minati/ae sunt	they threatened
pollicetur	he/she promises
pollicentur	they promise
pollicebitur	he/she will promise
pollicebuntur	they will promise
pollicitus/a est	he/she promised
polliciti/ae sunt	they promised
mentitur	he/she lies
mentiuntur	they lie
mentietur	he will lie
mentientur	they will lie
mentitus/a est	he/she lied
mentiti/ae sunt	they lied
patitur	he/she suffers
patiuntur	they suffer
patietur	he/she will suffer
patientur	they will suffer
passus/a est	he/she suffered
passi/ae sunt	they suffered

p.158 Exercises

1	*locutus*	having spoken	*loquor*
	profectus	having set out	*proficiscor*
	adeptus	having gained	*adipiscor*
	iratus	having become angry	*irascor*
	conatus	having tried	*conor*
	precatus	having prayed	*precor*
	suspicatus	having suspected	*suspicor*
	pollicitus	having promised	*polliceor*

hortatus	having encouraged	*hortor*
visus	having seemed	*videor*
egressus	having gone out	*egredior*
factus	having become	*fio*

2 (a) He caught the soldier after he (the soldier) had entered.
(b) The men thought a little, then came (after thinking a little the men came).
(c) He told a lot of lies, then went (he left after telling a heap of lies).
(d) Having advanced quickly from the city, the army soon pitched camp.
(e) Having said this she went out.

p.160 Exercises

1	*audacter*	boldly
	male	wickedly
	bene	well
	libere	freely
	magnopere	greatly
	multum	much
	celeriter	fast
	pulchre	beautifully
	paulum	slightly
2	*stulte*	stupidly
	bene	well
	fortiter	bravely
	longe	far
	similiter	in the same way
	saeue	wildly
	tacite	silently
	magnopere	greatly
	celeriter	fast/swiftly
	multum	much
	misere	unhappily

3 (the successful orator) will speak ... seriously, sternly, fiercely, powerfully, passionately, plentifully, bitterly, affably, gently, precisely, appealingly, kindly, sweetly, briefly and wittily.

p.162 Exercises

1 (a) The bold soldier wildly attacked the enemy – even though the latter was angry and had made lots of threats (the enemy was angry and made many threats, but the bold soldier attacked him wildly).

(b) The cavalry, after leaving their camp, quickly advanced to the city (leaving their camp, the cavalry quickly advanced to the city; the cavalry left their camp and quickly advanced to the city).

(c) The king got hold of a fast ship and fled far from his land.

(d) To his wife who had spoken much, her husband replied fiercely.

(e) When the ambassadors had spoken to the enemy, having returned to the camp, they reported their words to our leader.

(f) After encouraging his soldiers, the commander took himself boldly off to the battle.

(g) After suffering the ferocity of our cavalry, the enemy fled into their town and hid themselves away there.

2 (a) It's not living that's good, but living well.

(b) No one puts on a toga unless he's dead.

(c) The wealth of many exceptionally powerful people rules out loyal friendships: it's not just Fortune herself who is blind – she also generally renders blind those she has embraced.

pp.162–3 Reading

1 (a) So Amphitruo, having encouraged the soldiers at that time, went off to the battle.

(b) The commander spoke to the soldiers and, having promised (them) the plunder after the battle, gave the sign.

(c) The wife of Amphitruo, when she saw her husband in the street, left her house.

(d) To his wife, when she made many prayers and recalled the faithfulness of her husband, Amphitruo nevertheless made no reply.

(e) But the slave, having told many lies, easily deceived his master.

2 (a) ... to citizens who have gained leisure and peace.

(b) ... to the ambassadors after they had spoken these words.

(c) ... a band of slaves who had set out for the camp of the enemy.

(d) ... to that woman who had secretly followed her husband into the war.

(e) ... the commander, who had advanced to the enemy army.

(d) The soldiers spoke foul words ...

(b) The commander of the enemy uttered reproaches ...

(a) War seems to be the greatest evil ...

(e) The legions followed ...

(c) The masters killed ...

pp.163–4 Reading exercise/Test exercise

As the Teleboae had gained very much plunder in our land, our commander wanted to take revenge on them. So he set out with the army into the land of the Teleboae and waged war on them. But Amphitruo, a man of the utmost courage, speaking through representatives, instructed the Teleboae to give the plunder back. But the Teleboae, men of the utmost ferocity, saying much fiercely and threatening our army much, instructed Amphitruo to depart immediately. Accordingly a battle took place. Our commander, having prayed to the gods and having encouraged the army, led the soldiers into battle. The enemy advanced bravely, but at length we defeated them. However, Amphitruo received the enemy's representatives in the camp the following day, having achieved so famous a victory as this. The representatives of the enemy, when they had set out from the city and come to the camp, made a strong appeal to our commander and delivered themselves to his judgement.

p.164 English–Latin

1 (a) *dux noster, exercitum hortatus, signum dedit.*

(b) *Amphitruo per legatos hostes allocutus est.*

(c) *omnes sapientiam adepti pacem et otium quam bellum malunt.*

(d) *ea hora hostes a castris profecti sunt.*

(e) *plane mihi loqui conato hostes ferociter sunt minati.*

(f) *hominem sic locutum necauerunt.*

2 *Teleboae Amphitruoni per legatos allocuto* (or: *ubi Amphitruo eos per legatos allocutus est) haec responderunt: 'terram nostram adgressi estis. statim abite. nisi abibitis, pugnabimus.' haec dixerunt. Amphitruo autem, uir summa uirtute, cum exercitu e castris progessus, suos hortatus est. deinde in proelium duxit. ingens erat pugna. dux autem noster, uictoriam adeptus illustrem, iam domum regressus est.*

Section 3C

p.172 Exercises

1

about to enter	*intro*
about to shout	*clamo*
about to do	*facio*
about to have	*habeo*
about to advise	*moneo*
about to remain	*maneo*
about to hear	*audio*
about to lie	*mentior*
about to go out	*egredior*
about to lead	*duco*
about to capture	*capio*

2 future, past, future, future, past, future, future, future, past, future, future, past, future, past

3 *iturus, facturus, defensurus, redditurus, risurus, positurus, uisurus, iussurus, decepturus*

pp.172–3 Exercises

1 (a) But the very bad man has deceived me with tricks throughout all my most wretched life.
(b) Why therefore did he beat her fiercely with his fists?
(c) This year I finished this house with my (own) hands.
(d) Neither by cunning nor with tricks will you ever deceive the citizens.
(e) The utter scoundrel conducted the business very well for himself, with enormous misdeeds and very many crimes.
(f) Alcumena outdid all wives in her goodness and restraint.

2 (a) That slave is about to go into the house, isn't he?
(b) I am going to beat him with my fists at the same time.
(c) That man Sosia is about to act most foolishly, isn't he, if he wishes to enter this house?

(d) I very much want to deceive that slave for this night with my appearance.
(e) Sosia will never conquer me with his courage.
(f) What does he think is about to happen? For at this hour I am about to take his name away from him by my trickery.

p.174–5 Exercises

1 *stultius; melius; putidius; miserius; stultissime; optime; putidissime; miserrime; pulchrius; celerius; audacius; peius; pulcherrime; celerrime; audacissime; pessime*

2

2	*facillime*	most/very easily
	astutius	more cunningly
	optime	very well, best
	fortius	more bravely
	magis	more
	minime	least/very little
	pulcherrime	most beautifully

3 a man of the greatest courage
with the greatest courage
a slave of the greatest cunning
with the greatest cunning
with hands and feet
this year
with the same appearance
with my fists
at the same time

4 *eodem die*
uxor summa uirtute
summa uirtute
pugno meo
eodem anno
eisdem manibus
seruus summa audacia
dolo

5 (a) All the future is uncertain.
(b) We live among things destined to die.
(c) It is always difficult to talk about future events.
(d) The same goodness is in man and god.
(e) A way is made by violence.

p.175 Reading exercise/Test exercise

(a) My father has entrusted an enormous task to me at this time; for while he has decided to deceive Alcumena with Amphitruo's appearance, I am intending to drive the slave Sosia away from the house. I shall therefore go into the street, meaning to threaten that slave with destruction by my fists. I shall easily deceive him with my trickery because he seems to me to be a man of no intelligence. I shall therefore steal his name from him at the same time with my tricks. For it will please me to go up to him with the same appearance and the same voice.

(b) With his tricks and his cunning Mercury tricked Sosia as he was about to go into his master's house. For he did not allow Sosia to enter, although Amphitruo ordered him to tell Alcumena everything at that time. For Mercury looks after his father – that is, Jupiter. For Jupiter tricked Alcumena with the appearance of her husband in this house during this night. However, Mercury made himself like Sosia and took his name, with the same appearance and the same voice. Sosia at the last hardly trusted Mercury since he thought the god very like himself. And the slave thought this more easily because the god had the same hat, the same clothing, the same height, the same feet, the same chin, the same cheeks, the same lips, the same beard, the same nose, the same neck. Finally Sosia decided to consider himself Sosia because he knew himself well.

p.176 English–Latin

1 (a) *quid ille seruus acturus est?*
(b) *nonne proelium Alcumenae narraturus est?*
(c) *eodem tempore dolis et pugnis meis eum decepturus sum.*
(d) *huc enim ueni mortem ei minaturus.*
(e) *hoc dolo nomen ei auferre mihi placuit.*
(f) *ego nihil facilius, nihil melius, nihil celerius feci.*

2 MERC. *quis loquitur? eum, si inueniam, pugnis meis aggressurus sum.*

SOS. *mihi melius est tacere. si me illis pugnis tanget, certe tanti ero quanti murena.*

MERC. *quo iturus es, sceleste? quis es tu? ciuisne es?*

SOS. *seruus sum.*

MERC. *plura quam haec mihi dicere te uolo. quid est nomen tibi?*

SOS. *nomen mihi est Sosiae.*

MERC. *tu mentiris. mene dolis tuis decepturus es? nisi celeriter abibis, ego his pugnis te necabo.*

Section 3D

pp.183–4 Revision exercises

1

household	*famili-ae, -is*
eye	*ocul-o, -is*
plan/advice/judgement	*consili-o, -is*
mind/spirit/heart	*anim-o, -is*
dinner	*cen-ae, -is*
war	*bell-o, -is*
god	*de-o, -is*
crowd/mob	*turb-ae, -is*
victory	*uictori-ae, -is*
town	*oppid-o, -is*
booty	*praed-ae, -is*
father	*patr-i, -ibus*
respect	*honor-i, -ibus*
house/mansion	*aed-ibus*
brother	*fratr-i, -ibus*
sister	*soror-i, -ibus*
wife	*uxor-i, -ibus*
load/burden	*oner-i, -ibus*
man	*homin-i, -ibus*
citizen	*ciu-i, -ibus*
hand/band	*man-ui, -ibus*
day	*di-ei, -ebus*
night	*noct-i, -ibus*
work	*oper-i, -ibus*
head/source/fount	*capit-i, -ibus*

2	much	*mult-o, -ae, -o; -is*
	unhappy/wretched	*miser-o, -ae, -o; -is*
	bad/evil	*mal-o, -ae, -o; -is*
	my	*me-o, -ae, -o; -is*
	your (s.)	*tu-o, -ae, -o; -is*
	our	*nostr-o, -ae, -o; -is*
	your (pl.)	*uestr-o, -ae, -o; -is*
	every/all	*omn-i, -ibus*
	sad/gloomy	*trist-i, -ibus*
	huge	*ingent-i, -ibus*
	short/brief	*breu-i, -ibus*
	bold/brave	*audac-i, -ibus*
	this	*huic, his*

3	give	*do*	*dare*	*dedi*	*datus*
	stand	*sto*	*stare*	*steti*	*statum*
	order	*iubeo*	*iubere*	*iussi*	*iussus*
	possess/hold	*possideo*	*possidere*	*possedi*	*possessus*
	be	*sum*	*esse*	*fui*	fut. part.: *futurus*
	go/come	*eo*	*ire*	*ii*	*itum*
	bear/carry	*fero*	*ferre*	*tuli*	*latus*
	wish	*uolo*	*uelle*	*uolui*	—
	say/speak	*dico*	*dicere*	*dixi*	*dictus*
	lead/consider	*duco*	*ducere*	*duxi*	*ductus*
	take/capture	*capio*	*capere*	*cepi*	*captus*
	conduct	*gero*	*gerere*	*gessi*	*gestus*
	come	*uenio*	*uenire*	*ueni*	*uentum*
	defeat/conquer	*uinco*	*uincere*	*uici*	*uictus*

get/gain/acquire	*adipiscor*	*adipisci*	*adeptus*
go up to/attack	*adgredior*	*adgredi*	*adgressus*
speak	*loquor*	*loqui*	*locutus*
follow	*sequor*	*sequi*	*secutus*
set out	*proficiscor*	*proficisci*	*profectus*
encourage	*hortor*	*hortari*	*hortatus*

promise	*polliceor*	*polliceri*	*pollicitus*
lie	*mentior*	*mentiri*	*mentitus*
catch sight of	*conspicor*	*conspicari*	*conspicatus*
think/judge	*arbitror*	*arbitrari*	*arbitratus*
try	*conor*	*conari*	*conatus*

pp.184–5 Exercises

1 (a) *mihi* I may leave the house.
(b) *seruum* Mercury (has) attacked the slave with his fists.
(c) *huic* The slave obstructed this man (*or* got in his way).
(d) *tibi* I don't believe you.
(e) *illam* The man (*or*: her husband) loves her enormously.
(f) *uobis* That slave is threatening you. (*You threaten someone in the dative – p.183*)
(g) *patri* A good son always obeys his father. (p.182)
(h) *cenam* The cook is at present preparing dinner.
(i) *exercitui* My master is in charge of the army.
(j) *te* I instruct you to enter the house.
(k) *ei* The commander gave him this order ('ordered this to him').

2 (a) The cavalry are a hindrance to the legion.
(b) Alcumena is a major concern of Jupiter's. ('Alcumena is a great care to Jupiter.')
(c) This bad citizen is loathed by all decent people. ('... is an object of loathing to all good men.')
(d) Amphitruo was the salvation of his citizens.
(e) I will be a help to this city (*or*: I will go to the assistance of this city).
(f) This duty is a pleasure to me.
(g) This is your duty (this is something you are required to do).
(h) Alas! I will bring destruction upon all my family.
(i) This will do you no good (you'll regret this).
(j) The victory of Amphitruo benefits all citizens.

3 (a) I had a good son.
(b) My wife has a very large dowry.
(c) Our citizens had no help.
(d) No one has a good mistress.
(e) They have a son and a daughter.

4 (a) For a learned and educated man, living is thinking.
(b) No road to Virtue is impassable.
(c) Injustice cannot befall (be done to) the Wise Man.
(d) Men believe their eyes more than their ears.
(e) The man who mixes (Latin says 'mixed') useful with pleasant, wins ('won') every vote.

pp.185–6 Reading exercise/Test exercise

N.B. The key words that explain the dative have been italicized.

Sosia, when he comes to his (his master's) ship, will then *speak* to his master Amphitruo like this: 'I could not *report* your words to your wife, my lord, because a huge slave *threatened* me with his fists ('*threatened* fists to me'). He *obstructed* me fiercely. So *it was not possible* for me to go into the house. For that slave *was a very great hindrance* to your slave. So *it was necessary* for me to go back to you and *obey* his orders immediately, because I like how I look now ('my appearance is *pleasing* to me in this way, (namely) as it is'). This duty *was* not, as you promised, a *pleasure*, but a *great burden* to me.'

And Amphitruo will *reply* like this to his slave: 'What is that huge slave called (what *is the name* to that huge slave, what name does he have – dative of possession)?

Then Sosia (says): 'His name is Sosia ('to him the name is Sosia' – with Sosia attracted into the same case, dative, as 'him', see p.181. Strictly speaking Sosia complements the information about the name but 'Sosia' is so closely identified with the word 'him', it ends up in the same case as him, not in the same nominative case as *nomen*). For that slave *took from* me my name, my appearance, my voice, everything. I now have no name, except "Nobody".'

p.186 English–Latin

1 (a) *maximus mihi seruus obstitit.*
(b) *pulchra seni est filia/seni pulchra est filia/habet filiam pulchram senex/senex pulchram habet filiam/ ...*

(c) *militibus meis licet mihi imperare/militibus meis mihi imperare licet.*

(d) *Euclioni pecunia magnae uoluptati est/Euclioni pecunia ualde placet.*

(e) *malus ciuis omnibus odio est.*

(f) *omnes uolo imperiis meis parere/omnes imperiis meis parere mihi placet.*

(g) *hoc officium uxori oneri (magno) erit.*

(h) *dux, non milites, exercitui praeest.*

(i) *celerrime tibi in patriam regredi necesse est/necesse est tibi celerrime in patriam regredi.*

(j) *amantibus ita placet.*

2 JUP. *uale, uxor. necesse enim est mihi ad copias regredi.*

ALC. *quid tibi negoti est? tibine sum iam taedio?*

JUP. *immo, magnae mihi es uoluptati. sed ubi dux exercitui non praeest, milites officiis operam non dant.*

ALC. *noli abire, mi uir, plus te amare potero, si mihi parebis.*

JUP. *noli mihi obstare. mox regrediar ita ut uis. nunc tamen mihi abire placet. uale.*

Section Four

Section 4A

p.196 Exercises

1	*uideor*	*uidebar*	I was seeming	(like *pollicebar* – p.195)
	expugno	*expugnabam*	I was storming	(like *amabam* – p.194)
	fio	*fiebam*	I was being made	(like *capiebam* – p.194)
	peruenio	*perueniebam*	I was reaching	(like *audiebam* – p.194)
	sum	*eram*	I was	
	conor	*conabar*	I was trying	(like *minabar* – p.195)
	iubeo	*iubebam*	I was ordering	(like *habebam* – p.194)
	reduco	*reducebam*	I was leading back	(like *dicebam* – p.194)
	irascor	*irascebar*	I was getting angry	(like *loquebar* – p.195)
	facio	*faciebam*	I was making	(like *capiebam* – p.194)

2	*tenebas*	you (s.) were holding	*tenebatis*
	loquebantur	they were speaking	*loquebatur*
	praeerat	he was in charge	*praeerant*
	minabamini	you (pl.) were threatening	*minabaris*
	imperabam	I was ordering	*imperabamus*
	ueniebatis	you (pl.) were coming	*ueniebas*

audebant	they were daring	*audebat*
obliuiscebaris	you (s.) were forgetting	*obliuiscebamini*
audiebat	he was listening	*audiebant*
patiebamur	we were suffering	*patiebar*
auferebamus	we were taking away	*auferebam*
sequebar	I was following	*sequebamur*

3

I used to think	*arbitrabar*
he was abandoning	*relinquebat*
they were throwing	*coniciebant*
we used to follow	*sequebamur*
you (s.) were reporting	*deferebas*
she was going out	*exibat*
they were accustomed	*solebant*
you (pl.) were	*eratis*
we were stating strongly	*affirmabamus*

4	**Present**	**Future**	**Imperfect**	**Perfect**
sentio	*sentit*	*sentiet*	*sentiebat*	*sensit*
	sentiunt	*sentient*	*sentiebant*	*senserunt*
minor	*minatur*	*minabitur*	*minabatur*	*minatus est*
	minantur	*minabuntur*	*minabantur*	*minati sunt*
ueto	*uetat*	*uetabit*	*uetabat*	*uetuit*
	uetant	*uetabunt*	*uetabant*	*uetuerunt*
tollo	*tollit*	*tollet*	*tollebat*	*sustulit*
	tollunt	*tollent*	*tollebant*	*sustulerunt*
eo	*it*	*ibit*	*ibat*	*iuit (or iit)*
	eunt	*ibunt*	*ibant*	*iuerunt (or ierunt)*
sum	*est*	*erit*	*erat*	*fuit*
	sunt	*erunt*	*erant*	*fuerunt*
audeo	*audet*	*audebit*	*audebat*	*ausus est*
	audent	*audebunt*	*audebant*	*ausi sunt*
adipiscor	*adipiscitur*	*adipiscetur*	*adipiscebatur*	*adeptus est*
	adipiscuntur	*adipiscentur*	*adipiscebantur*	*adepti sunt*
uideor	*uidetur*	*uidebitur*	*uidebatur*	*uisus est*
	uidentur	*uidebuntur*	*uidebantur*	*uisi sunt*
teneo	*tenet*	*tenebit*	*tenebat*	*tenuit*
	tenent	*tenebunt*	*tenebant*	*tenuerunt*

	Present	**Future**	**Imperfect**	**Perfect**
adgredior	*adgreditur*	*adgredietur*	*adgrediebatur*	*adgressus est*
	adgrediuntur	*adgredientur*	*adgrediebantur*	*adgressi sunt*
mentior	*mentitur*	*mentietur*	*mentiebatur*	*mentitus est*
	mentiuntur	*mentientur*	*mentiebantur*	*mentiti sunt*
accuso	*accusat*	*accusabit*	*acusabat*	*accusauit*
	accusant	*accusabunt*	*accusabant*	*accusauerunt*
colo	*colit*	*colet*	*colebat*	*coluit*
	colunt	*colent*	*colebant*	*coluerunt*

5 Imperfects are underlined.

loquar	future
sentiebat	he was feeling
amabit	future
negabat	he was denying
solebunt	future
audebant	they were daring
ponam	future
tollebatis	you (pl.) were removing
reliquit	perfect
habebit	future
tacebant	they were silent
opinaberis	future
arbitrabaris	you (s.) were thinking
expugnant	present
repellebas	you (s.) were driving back
iudicabatis	you were judging
coniecistis	perfect

If you got any of these wrong, check which conjugation the verb belongs to.

Exercises p.197

1 *istius:* *serui, feminae, templi, manus, rei, custodis, impetus* (gen. sing. masc./fem./neut.)

ista: *lege, sacerdote* (*sacerdos*, priest, can be fem.) (abl. sing. fem.)

	isti:	*serui, uirtuti, manui, negotio, milites* (dat. sing. masc./fem./neut. *or* nom. pl. masc.)
	ista:	*femina res simulacra* (nom. sing. fem. *or* nom./acc. pl. neut.)

2	*serui*	*istius* (gen. sing.); *isti* (nom. pl.)
	negotio	*isti* (dat. sing.); *isto* (abl. sing.)
	uirtuti	*isti* (dat. sing.)
	custodibus	*istis* (dat./abl. pl.)
	manus	*istius* (gen. sing.); *istae* (nom. pl.); *istas* (acc. pl.)

p.198 Exercises

1	*seruorum quorundam*	gen. pl.	of certain slaves
	custodi cuidam	dat. sing.	to a certain guard
	signa quaedam	nom./acc. pl. (neuter)	certain statues
	clamores quosdam	acc. pl.	certain shouts
	dolo quodam	abl. sing.	by a certain trick
	iudicibus quibusdam	dat. pl. *or* abl. pl.	for certain judges *or* by, with, from

2	*cuiusdam:*	*templi sacerdotis manus* (gen. sing. masc./fem./neut.)
	quaedam:	*femina res negotia leges loca* (nom. sing./pl. fem. *or* nom./acc. pl. neut.)
	quidam:	*custos nuntius pueri milites magistratus iudices* (nom. sing./pl. masc.)

p.201 Exercises

1

	Present	Perfect	Future
sum	*esse*	*fuisse*	*futurus esse*
accuso	*accusare*	*accusauisse*	*accusaturus esse*
expugno	*expugnare*	*expugnauisse*	*expugnaturus esse*
confirmo	*confirmare*	*confirmauisse*	*confirmaturus esse*
iubeo	*iubere*	*iussisse*	*iussurus esse*
reduco	*reducere*	*reduxisse*	*reducturus esse*
tollo	*tollere*	*sustulisse*	*sublaturus esse*
conicio	*conicere*	*coniecisse*	*coniecturus esse*
egredior	*egredi*	*egressus esse*	*egressurus esse*
mentior	*mentiri*	*mentitus esse*	*mentiturus esse*
uenio	*uenire*	*uenisse*	*uenturus esse*
eo	*ire*	*iuisse* (or *iisse)*	*iturus esse*

2

passurus esse	future	*patior*
loqui	present	*loquor*
amauisse	perfect	*amo*
sentire	present	*sentio*
habiturus esse	future	*habeo*
sustulisse	perfect	*tollo*
minatus esse	perfect	*minor*
uelle	present	*uolo*
iturus esse	future	*eo*
expugnare	present	*expugno*
secutus esse	perfect	*sequor*
poscere	present	*posco*
posuisse	perfect	*pono*
adeptus esse	perfect	*adipiscor*
iudicasse	perfect	*iudico*
repperturus esse	future	*reperio*
deferre	present	*defero*

3	to seem	*uideri*
	to have forbidden	*uetuisse*
	to be about to think	*arbitraturus esse*
	to report	*deferre*
	to have found	*inuenisse*
	to be about to remove	*ablaturus esse*
	to follow	*sequi*
	to have remembered	*meminisse*
	to be about to lie	*mentiturus esse*
	to promise	*promittere*
	to have spoken	*locutus esse*
	to be about to forget	*obliturus esse*

4	*solitus es*	2nd sing. perf.	*solere*
	detulistis	2nd pl. perf.	*deferre*
	confirmauere (= confirmauerunt)	3rd pl. perf.	*confirmare*
	affirmare	present infinitive	*affirmare*
	sequere	2nd sing. pres. (or imperative)	*sequi*
	coluisse	perfect infinitive	*colere*
	puta	imperative	*putare*
	hortatus esse	perfect infinitive	*horti*
	reperire	present infinitive	*reperire*
	mentire	imperative	*mentiri*
	accusaturus esse	future infinitive	*accusare*
	ausus est	3rd sing. perf.	*audere*
	repellere	present infinitive	*repellere*
	loquere	2nd sing. pres. (or imperative)	*loqui*
	expugnauisse	perfect infinitive	*expugnare*
	auditurus esse	future infinitive	*audire*
	deferebat	3rd sing. imperf.	*deferre*
	iudicaturus esse	future infinitive	*indicare*

p.203 Exercises

1 (a) Cicero states strongly that the people of Agrigentum have a statue of Hercules.

(b) The people of Agrigentum were saying that Verres had not been a good praetor.

(c) The story was that that man's slaves had entered the temple and had removed the statue.

(d) Cicero said that a certain messenger had announced all of this to the people of Agrigentum.

(e) I think that that man will always lie to you.

(f) Cicero was of the opinion that no one would ever commit worse crimes than that man.

(g) Verres used to send his slaves to the temples, take gold from citizens by force, show favour to his friends, even against the law, and embrace all crimes.

(h) I hear that Verres will report the name of a certain slave.

(i) Verres, because he did not want to be incriminated, ordered a certain friend to lie.

(j) I know that Verres was accustomed to accuse innocent men.

(k) Surely you have never heard more wicked crimes, gentlemen of the jury?

(l) Verres is a most wicked man, is he not?

(m) I heard that the people of Agrigentum had made an attack on Verres' slaves.

2 (a) Reason tells us that the gods exist.

(b) The outcome taught (us) that fortune favours the brave.

(c) I am a human being: I think there is nothing to do with humanity that does not concern me. (*Humani* is missing from the Latin sentence.)

(d) They say that Democritus was never seen in public without a smile.

(e) A young man hopes that he will live for a long time.

(f) Renown is a fickle and unstable thing.

(g) Recently the illness of a certain friend of mine reminded me that we are at our best when we are ill. For what sick man does avarice or lust ever trouble?

(h) Here, where Rome now stands, an uncut wood used to grow green; (the site of) such a great project was pasture for a few oxen.

pp.204–6 Reading exercises

Translations only. Where there is ambiguity, the more likely translation is given first.

1 (a) ... that the slaves will storm the temple.

(b) ... that Verres has sent the slaves to the temple.
(*or*: ... that the slaves have sent Verres to the temple.)

(c) ... that the people of Assorus worship Chrysas (the river-god).
(*or*: ... that Chrysas worships the people of Assorus.)

(d) ... that Verres will accuse me.
(*or*: ... that I will accuse Verres.)

(e) ... that they (he, she, *or* it) love the statues.
(*or*: ... that the statues love themselves.)

(f) ... that Scipio was a man of the greatest kindness.

(g) ... that the women have spotted everything.

(h) ... that that man will leave the city by night.

(i) ... that a great uproar had taken place.

(j) ... that he is going home.

2 The controlling verb is in **bold**; the accusative and infinitive is underlined.

Cicero templum esse apud Agrigentinos **dixit**. *id* **affirmauit** *non longe a foro esse. in hoc templum intrauisse* **dixit** *Verris seruos. eos Verrem misisse Cicero* **opinatus est**. *Verres autem se hoc fecisse* **negabat**. *fama* **percrebrescebat** *Verris seruos in templum* **ingressos esse** *et custodes templum defendere conatos esse. magnum clamorem custodes fecisse* **putauit** *Cicero; Agrigentinos igitur ex urbe progressos esse et ad templum uenisse. fugisse tum seruos Verris* **affirmauit**. *Cicero* **negabat** *umquam se scelera peiora auditurum esse.*

Translation

Cicero said that there was a temple belonging to (amongst) the people of Agrigentum. He declared that it was not far from the forum. He said it was this temple Verres' slave had entered. Cicero was of the opinion that Verres had sent them. Verres however denied that he had done so. The story spread abroad that Verres' slaves had gone into the temple and that the guards had tried to defend the temple. Cicero thought that the guards had caused a great commotion; and that the people of Agrigentum had therefore come forth from the city and had come to the temple. He declared that, at that point, the slaves of Verres had fled. Cicero said that he would never hear worse crimes.

3	(a)	acc. + infin.	They said that that could not happen.
	(b)	prolative infin.	He did not want you to do this.
	(c)	prolative infin.	I order you to remove the statue of Chrysas.
	(d)	acc. + infin.	He was declaring that the slaves had tried to kill him.
	(e)	acc. + infin.	The story was that Verres had removed the statue.
	(f)	prolative infin.	Gentlemen of the jury, all the people of Agrigentum were wanting me to prosecute Verres.

4 *Cicero dicit templum apud Agrigentinos esse non longe a foro. affirmat ibi esse simulacrum Herculis pulcherrimum. negat se pulchrius simulacrum quam illud umquam conspicatum esse. fama est ad hoc templum Verrem repente nocte seruos quosdam armatos misisse. dicit hos concurrisse et templum expugnauisse. affirmat custodes templi clamauisse et seruis obsistere templumque defendere conatos esse. dicit eos mox et peiora et scelestiora audituros esse.*

p.206 Reading exercise/Test exercise

I hear that there is a shrine of Ceres belonging to the people of Catina. Everyone knows that men are not allowed to enter that shrine. The story goes that women and young girls usually carry out the sacrifices there. Many people declare that in that shrine there used to be a very ancient statue of Ceres. Cicero said that Verres' slaves had removed this statue from that place at night; and that it had seemed to everybody to be a most dreadful business. Cicero said that Verres had then ordered a certain friend to find and accuse someone. For he (Cicero) said that he (Verres) did not want to be incriminated. Cicero declared that the friend had put forward the name of a certain slave, had accused the slave, and had provided false witnesses against him. However, he also stated that the senate of the people of Catina had called the priestesses and had asked them about the whole affair. Cicero said that all the priestesses had seen everything, and that the senate had said the slave was innocent. Cicero thought that the members of the jury had never heard worse crimes, but that soon they would hear worse.

p.206 English–Latin

1 (a) *arbitror Verrem hoc fecisse.*

(b) *Cicero dixit seruos in templum intrauisse.*

(c) *multi ciues ad urbem ueniebant, negotium faciebant, domum regrediebantur.*

(d) *amicus Verris nomen cuiusdam serui detulit.*

(e) *nos omnes scimus istum scelestum esse.*

(f) *num arbitraris seruos simulacrum sustulisse?*

(g) *Cicero uir optimus erat, amicos libenter defendebat, numquam scelerum hostium nostrorum obliuiscebatur.*

(h) *Cicero arbitratur iudices numquam peius scelus audituros esse.*

2 *Syracusanis lex est de sacerdotio Iouis. Cicero dicit hanc legem Syracusanos iubere tres uiros creare; Syracusanis sortiri necesse esse; unum ex tribus sacerdotem fieri. affirmat Verrem amico cuidam, Theomnasto nomine, sacerdotium dare uoluisse; Syracusanos negauisse; Verrem dolo rem perfecisse.*

Section 4B

p.216 Exercises

1 (a)

comite claro	*comitibus claris*
calamitate magna	*calamitatibus magnis*
conuiuio Graeco	*conuiuiis Graecis*
amico nobili	*amicis nobilibus*
magistratu innocenti	*magistratibus innocentibus*
forma turpi	*formis turpibus*
re Romana	*rebus Romanis*

(b) The ablatives are: *comitibus, Asia, conuiuiis, sermone, ui, amico, diebus, homine turpi, uiro nobili, manu celeri*

(c)

ingenti	dat./abl. sing.	*templo, uirgine, cura*
audacibus	dat./abl. pl.	*feminis, sacerdotibus*
sola	abl. sing. fem.	*uirtute*
magnis	dat./abl. pl.	*pueris, manibus*
tanto	dat./abl. sing. masc./neut.	*proelio, praetore*
longiore	abl. sing.	*periculo, uia*

N.B. Most third declension nouns have ablative singular ending in *-e*. If you have made any mistakes, check carefully the declension of the nouns and adjectives.

2 N.B. The underlined words below relate to the Reading exercise on *GVE* pp.219–20, which you will come to later.

(a) The man was much better than all the others.

(b) He said that he had not killed the man with the utmost force.
(*literally*, He denied himself to have killed ...)

(c) That man beat the door with rocks.

(d) Cicero asserted that the Agrigentini were brave men.
(*literally*, men of great courage)

(e) Praetors, very serious men (*literally*, men of the utmost seriousness), do not enjoy parties.

(f) The Lampsaceni used to conduct their business in the Greek manner.

(g) Greeks prefer to spend their life in leisure and peace (rather) than in war and disasters.

(h) Cicero thought that Verres was worse than the other praetors.
(*literally*, ... thought Verres to be...)

(i) The story was that Verres' slaves had used the greatest violence.
(*utor* takes the ablative)

(j) At that time Ianitor came to Verres with all speed and tried to detain him with many words.

pp.217–8 Exercises

1	*alius*	nom. sing. masc./gen. sing. masc./fem./neut.	*comes, hospitis, calamitatis*
	alii	dat. sing./nom. pl. masc.	*Lampsaceno, sermones, ianuae*
	alia	nom. sing. fem. *or* nom./acc. pl. neut.	*conuiuia, uirgo*
	alia	abl. sing. fem.	*calamitate*
	aliqua	nom. sing. fem.	*mulier*
	aliqua	abl. sing. fem.	*re, serua*

2 (a) Different people say different things. (*Note 1 p.217*)
(b) Some were Lampsaceni, the others were Agrigentini.
(c) Different people are making an attack on the town in different places.
(d) Some ran from the fields, others from the town. (*Note 2 p.217*)
(e) Someone will say something.
(f) But who is calling? Some magistrate? No one.
(g) Catiline, are you hesitating to go away to some country?
(h) Verres left the house with some companion.

p.219 Exercises

1	*ipsi*	dat. sing./masc. pl. nom.	*calamitati, consules, conuiuio, nuntii*
	ipsa	nom. sing. fem. *or* nom./acc. pl. neut.	*grauitas, signa, simulacra*
	ipsa	abl. sing. fem.	*grauitate*

2	*ipsi uoluere (= erunt)*	they themselves wanted
	signum ipsum	the statue itself
	ipsae clamarunt (= auerunt)	the women themselves shouted
	consilio ipso	by the plan itself
	ipsi homini pepercerunt	they themselves spared the man *or* they spared the man himself (*parco* takes the dative; *ipsi* = dat. sing. *or* nom. pl. masc.)
	ipsa laetitia	the joy itself
	obsecrarunt ipsi oraruntque (= averunt)	they themselves begged and prayed
	noli ipsam retinere	*literally,* don't keep the girl herself

3 (a) No one can be of a calm mind.
(b) The wise man conquers Fortune with courage.
(c) Alas, Fortune, who is a more cruel god to us than you? (*te* = ablative of comparison)
(d) That man enjoys riches the most who least needs riches. (*fruor* takes the ablative)
(e) Alas, how difficult it is not to betray a crime by one's expression.
(f) Silver is cheaper than gold, gold is cheaper than virtue.
(g) An honourable death is better than a shameful life.
(h) Always something new out of Africa.
(i) The whole life of man is nothing other than the journey to death.
(j) Nature shows different routes to different people. (*or* ... one route to one man, a different one to another.)

p.219 Reading

The ablative phrases are indicated by the underlining in the answers to p.216 question 2 given on p.163 above.

(a)	*multo*	ablative of measure of difference
	omnibus aliis	comparison after *melior*
(b)	*summa ui*	describing how (ablative of manner)
(c)	*saxis*	instrument – 'with which'
(d)	no ablative phrase	

(e)	*summa grauitate*	describing the praetors (ablative of description)
	conuiuiis	*fruor* takes the ablative
(f)	*more Graeco*	describing how they acted
(g)	*otio et pace* and *bello et calamitatibus*	describing how they prefer to live
(h)	*ceteris praetoribus*	comparison after *peiorem*
(i)	*summa ui*	*utor* takes the ablative
(j)	*eo tempore*	time when
	summa celeritate	describes how he came (ablative of manner)
	multis uerbis	instrument – 'with which'

p.220 Reading exercise/Test exercise

In the Hellespont, judges, you know that there is a town more famous and more noble than the other towns of Asia, called Lampsacus (Lampsacus by name). I assert that the Lampsaceni themselves are peaceful (quiet) men. They spend their life in the Greek manner. For they prefer to make use of leisure and peace (rather) than to spend their life in wars and disasters. That man arrived at Lampsacus at a certain time (on one occasion). The Lampsaceni took him to Ianitor, a very important man. That man however soon said that he would move to a certain Philodamus. For Philodamus had at home a very beautiful daughter. Judges, you know that Verres always strongly pursued beautiful women in all ways and at all times. Ianitor thought that he had offended Verres in some way and began to detain him with the utmost force. Verres therefore sent Rubrius to Philodamus, using a very bad (wicked) plan, because Philodamus was a man of great repute among the Lampsaceni and was used to receiving praetors and consuls, not their friends. But Verres ordered Rubrius to bring Philodamus by force. Philodamus, because he did not want to appear unwilling, prepared a party (and) ordered Rubrius to invite all his friends. They came with all speed; they reclined at table; at first they drank in the Greek manner (but) soon in larger goblets. They enjoyed the party at this time with happy conversations (with joy and conversations). But soon Rubrius said, 'Philodamus, call your daughter'. But he, a man of the utmost rectitude, was angry. He said that women should not recline at a party with men. An enormous uproar occurred through the house. When the Lampsaceni heard the disorder, they gathered at night at Philodamus' house with the utmost speed.

Next day, however, they set out to Verres' lodging. They began to attack (beat) the door with swords (iron) and rocks (and) at the same time to put fire around it. But the Lampsaceni spared Verres because some citizens said that this would be better for them than to kill a Roman praetor.

pp.220–21 English–Latin

1 (a) *Verres Rubrio peior erat.*

(b) *Lampsaceni pace et otio fruebantur.*

(c) *Philodamus erat uir summae grauitatis* (gen.), *Verres summa cupiditate* (abl.).

(d) *coqui conuiuium sermone et laetitia parabant.*

(e) *Verres et comites more Graeco bibebant.*

(f) *Lampsaceni ianuam pugnis pulsabant et eodem tempore summa uoce clamabant.*

2 *Philodamus erat uir summa grauitate, aliis tamen semper multo hospitalior. Rubrium et comites ad conuiuium inuitauit. omnes summa celeritate peruenerunt. sermone et laetitia bibebant. subito autem Rubrius Philodamum iussit filiam uocare. Philodamus autem negabat se eam uocaturum esse. tumultus tum erat.*

Section 4C

pp.228–9 Exercises

1

conatus/-a/-um eram	I had tried
excogitaueram	I had devised
uisus/-a/-um eram	I had seemed
monueram	I had warned
usus/-a/-um eram	I had used
feceram	I had made
afueram	I had been away
collegeram	I had collected
commoueram	I had (re)moved

2

you (pl.) had begged	*oraueras*
you (s.) had caught sight of	*conspicati eratis*
he had moved	*commouerant*
they had urged	*hortata erat*
I had spared	*peperceramus*
she had remembered	*recordatae erant*
we had welcomed	*receperam*
I had embraced	*amplexi eramus*
you (s.) had cut down	*cecideratis*
we had forgotten	*oblitus eram*
they had ignored	*neglexerat*
you (pl.) had advanced	*progressus eras*

3

constitueram
passus eras
reuocauerant
recordati erant
cognouerat
adepta erat
excogitaueramus
amplexi eratis
collegeramus
commoueras

4

Pres.	**Fut.**	**Imperf.**	**Perf.**	**Pluperf.**
reuocat	*reuocabit*	*reuocabat*	*reuocauit*	*reuocauerat*
reuocant	*reuocabunt*	*reuocabant*	*reuocauerunt*	*reuocauerant*
tenet	*tenebit*	*tenebat*	*tenuit*	*tenuerat*
tenent	*tenebunt*	*tenebant*	*tenuerunt*	*tenuerant*
arbitratur	*arbitrabitur*	*arbitrabatur*	*arbitratus/-a/-um est*	*arbitratus/-a/-um erat*
arbitrantur	*arbitrabuntur*	*arbitrabantur*	*arbitrati/-ae/-a sunt*	*arbitrati/-ae/-a erant*
uidetur	*uidebitur*	*uidebatur*	*uisus/-a/-um est*	*uisus/-a/-um erat*
uidentur	*uidebuntur*	*uidebantur*	*uisi/-ae/-a sunt*	*uisi/-ae/-a erant*
neglegit	*negleget*	*neglegebat*	*neglexit*	*neglexerat*
neglegunt	*neglegent*	*neglegebant*	*neglexerunt*	*neglexerant*
sentit	*sentiet*	*sentiebat*	*sensit*	*senserat*
sentiunt	*sentient*	*sentiebant*	*senserunt*	*senserant*
utitur	*utetur*	*utebatur*	*usus/-a/-um est*	*usus/-a/-um erat*
utuntur	*utentur*	*utebantur*	*usi/-ae/-a sunt*	*usi/-ae/-a erant*
patitur	*patietur*	*patiebatur*	*passus/-a/-um est*	*passus/-a/-um erat*
patiuntur	*patientur*	*patiebantur*	*passi/-ae/-a sunt*	*passi/-ae/-a erant*
fit	*fiet*	*fiebat*	*factus/-a/-um est*	*factus/-a/-um erat*
fiunt	*fient*	*fiebant*	*facti/-ae/-a sunt*	*facti/-ae/-a erant*
non uult	*nolet*	*nolebat*	*noluit*	*noluerat*
nolunt	*nolent*	*nolebant*	*noluerunt*	*noluerant*
est	*erit*	*erat*	*fuit*	*fuerat*
sunt	*erunt*	*erant*	*fuerunt*	*fuerant*
colligit	*colliget*	*colligebat*	*collegit*	*collegerat*
colligunt	*colligent*	*colligebant*	*collegerunt*	*collegerant*
constituit	*constituet*	*constituebat*	*constituit*	*constituerat*
constituunt	*constituent*	*constituebant*	*constituerunt*	*constituerant*

5 impf; he had called back; perf; you (s.) had collected; fut; pres; they had read through; fut; you (s.) had tried; perf; you (pl.) had been; perf; they had gone out; perf; pres; fut; we had killed.

pp.231–2 Exercises

1 The antecedent is underlined.

(a) Diodorus used to have small <u>cups</u>, which Mentor had made.
(b) <u>The letter</u>, which he had written, soon arrived in Sicily.
(c) He was calling back <u>the men</u> who had asserted that they were in Rome.
(d) <u>The thing</u> which you have devised is criminal.
(e) <u>Diodorus</u>, whom Verres knew had certain very beautiful cups, had gone away.
(f) Diodorus was born from a noble <u>family</u> which had never become well-known.

2 (a) *quem:* He was a man whom all the women used to love.
(b) *cui:* She was a woman to whom every man was pleasing.
(c) *quam:* The young girl, whom Verres had wanted to love, was noble.
(d) *qui:* Many men, who had become the companions of Verres, were the sons of noblemen.
(e) *quae:* Mentor had made the small cups which the companions of Verres had caught sight of.
(f) *quorum:* Many men, whose greed the good citizens had thought was very great, were going to Verres.
(g) *quod:* The companions of Verres removed from the temple the statue which that man had dared to desire. (Note misprint *cupire* for *cupere* in the Latin in *GVE*.)
(h) *quos:* The companions whom Verres had brought away with him to Lilybaeum, had caught sight of the cups of Diodorus.

3 *quae: poculis* (neut. pl.)
quem: seruus (masc. sing.)
cuius: genus (neut. sing.)
qui: filio (masc. sing.)
quibus: fana (neut. pl.)

4 (a) and when he had heard it ...
(b) and when he had told these things ...
(c) and when they had recalled these women ...
(d) and when they had caught sight of them ...
(e) and when he had threatened him ...

pp.234–5 Exercises

1 (a) A young girl of excellent reputation
(b) When Cicero and Antonius were consuls
(c) Under my leadership
(d) Young girls born from a noble family
(e) He removed the gold out of boldness and greed
(f) From Rome
(g) At home
(h) From Lilybaeum
(i) In the whole province
(j) In the absence of the praetors

2 (a) *uir magnae uirtutis/uir magna uirtute*
(b) *Verre praetore*
(c) *te duce*
(d) *puer genere nobili natus*
(e) *hoc modo cupiditate*
(f) *Romae*
(g) *domo*
(h) *Lilybaeum*
(i) *tota Sicilia*
(j) *ceteris absentibus*

3 (a) He who has much desires more.
(b) The poor man is not he who has too little but he who desires more.
(c) He who has begun (it) has half the deed (i.e. is half-way there).
(d) Fortune snatches nothing away except what she has given.
(e) It is sweet to remember what was hard to endure.
(f) Diaulus was recently a doctor, now he's an undertaker; what he does as an undertaker, he had also done as a doctor.

p.235 Reading exercise/Test exercise

That man by his greed drove out from the province Diodorus of Malta, who had left Malta long before and at that time was living in Lilybaeum. He had been a man of great respect among the people of Lilybaeum, who had got to know that he was a man of the greatest goodness. But in Verres' praetorship, he lacked a home for a period of almost three years because of certain beautiful cups which he used to have. For the companions, whom that man had brought with him when he came to the province, had announced to him that Diodorus had these cups; and when he had got to know this, inflamed by greed, he had summoned Diodorus to him and had demanded the cups. However, Diodorus, who was unwilling to lose the cups, had asserted that they were in Malta in the hands of a close relative. But when Verres had written a letter to that relative, in which he kept on demanding the cups, the man had said that he had sent them to Lilybaeum within the last few days. Meanwhile Diodorus had departed from Lilybaeum.

pp.235–6 English–Latin

1 (a) *Diodorus, qui multa pocula pulchra habebat, Lilybaeo Romam abierat.*

(b) *Verre praetore, tota prouincia uiri facta scelesta excogitare poterant.*

(c) *Verres, qui genere nobili natus erat, semper cupiditate potius quam uirtute agebat.*

(d) *comites, quos Verres secum ad prouinciam duxerat, erant scelesti.*

2 *quae ubi Verres audiuit, insania Diodorum absentem accusare constituit. tota prouincia res clara erat. fama erat Verrem cupiditate argenti uirum innocentem absentem accusauisse. Diodorus, qui hoc tempore Romae erat, omnia quae audiuerat suis patronis narrauit. quae ubi pater Verris audiuit, litteras isti misit. quibus in litteris narrabat omnes tota urbe scire Verrem esse scelestum. quae ubi Verres perlegit, cupiditatem timore potius quam pudore repressit.*

Section 4D

pp.247–8 Exercises

1	*captum iri*	to be about to be (to be going to be) captured
	liberatum iri	to be about to be (to be going to be) set free
	iussum iri	to be about to be (to be going to be) ordered
	ablatum iri	to be about to be (to be going to be) taken away
	repertum iri	to be about to be (to be going to be) found

2 (a) Verres said the robbers would be captured.
(b) Verres said that the Roman citizens would not be freed.
(c) Verres asserts that the cups of Diodorus will be taken away.
(d) Diodorus says that the cups will not be found by Verres.
(e) Verres said that his friends would be ordered to find the cups.
(f) I shall go to see if he is at home.
(g) Maecenas goes to play, Virgil and I to sleep.

pp.249–51 Exercises

1	*liberor*	*liberamur*	I am freed etc.
	liberaris	*liberamini*	
	liberatur	*liberantur*	
	adiuuabar	*adiuuabamur*	I was being helped etc.
	adiuuabaris	*adiuuabamini*	
	adiuuabatur	*adiuuabantur*	
	iubebor	*iubebimur*	I shall be ordered etc.
	iubeberis	*iubebimini*	
	iubebitur	*iubebuntur*	
	uideor	*uidemur*	I am seen/I seem etc.
	uideris	*uidemini*	
	uidetur	*uidentur*	
	latus eram	*lati eramus*	I had been carried etc.
	latus eras	*lati eratis*	
	latus erat	*lati erant*	

caesus sum	*caesi sumus*	I have been killed/
caesus es	*caesi estis*	I was killed etc.
caesus est	*caesi sunt*	
reuocari		to be called back
confirmatus esse		to have been confirmed
recipior	*recipimur*	I am received etc.
reciperis	*recipimini*	
recipitur	*recipiuntur*	
dicar	*dicemur*	I shall be said etc.
diceris	*dicemini*	
dicetur	*dicentur*	

2 she followed (deponent)
he is accused (passive)
they were taken away (passive)
he was left (passive)
he is carried (passive)
he speaks (deponent)
he lied (deponent)
he used to catch sight of (deponent)
he will consider (deponent)
he will try (deponent)
it will be told (passive)
it was announced (passive)
it was seen (passive)
it dared (deponent)

3 *capietur*
liberari
feriebantur
ablatum erat
reuocatus esse
perlectum est

4 (a) The ship was not captured by our fleet.
(b) The news was announced to Verres by a messenger.
(c) The ship was brought to Syracuse by the sailors.
(d) The craftsmen were taken away by Verres.
(e) The pirates were executed with an axe by the Romans.

5 (a) Nothing had been said by Verres.
(b) The ship was captured by a pirate.
(c) Young men are sent by Verres to Rome.
(d) The pirates' ship was taken away by our men.
(e) My treasure will be given to friends.
(f) It was announced to Verres that the ship had been captured and that the pirates were being killed with an axe.

6 (a) *homines a Romanis defendebantur.*
(b) *numerus praedonum a te cognitus est.*
(c) *pecunia a Verre data est.*
(d) *ciues Romani a Verre securi feriuntur.*
(e) *nautae ab illo liberabuntur.*
(f) *pocula a Diodoro ablata erant.*

p.251 Reading exercise/Test exercise

It was announced to Verres that, with Publius Caesetius and Publius Tadius in command, a certain pirate ship had been captured, and that the ship was full of very handsome young men, silver and clothes. Verres ordered the ship to be brought to Syracuse by the sailors. Then punishment was expected by everyone. But although the old men were executed immediately, the handsome young men however were taken away by him and given to his friends. Nobody had thought the pirates would be freed. However this was done by Verres.

But afterwards a much more wicked deed was done by him. For in the place of the pirates who had been freed, Verres began to substitute Roman citizens, who had previously been thrown into prison. Although they were known by many, they were still killed with an axe.

p.251 English–Latin

1 (a) *nauis a Romanis inuenta est.*
(b) *pecunia Verri a praedonibus dabatur.*
(c) *iuuenes Romam mittuntur.*
(d) *nuntiatum erat nauem captam esse et Syracusas appelli.*
(e) *nemo praedones captum iri senserat.*
(f) *Verres Romae accusabitur.*

2 *Syracusani rationem habebant praedonum qui necati erant. quae ratio habita erat ex numero remorum qui capti erant. magnus numerus praedonum deerat, quod multi a Verre liberati erant. ciues autem Romani in praedonum locum substituti sunt. Verres illos milites Sertorianos fuisse arguit. quamquam a multis Syracusanis cogniti erant securi percussi sunt.*

Section 4E

pp.262–3 Exercises

1	*reuocans, reuocantis*	calling back
	incendens, incendentis	setting fire to
	accipiens, accipientis	receiving
	sentiens, sentientis	feeling
	iubens, iubentis	ordering
	adipiscens, adipiscentis	getting
	egrediens, egredientis	going out
	fruens, fruentis	enjoying
	recordans, recordantis	remembering
	exiens, exeuntis	going out

2	*inspicienti:*	*seruae, uiro*	(dat. sing.)
		muliere	(abl. sing.)
	accedentem:	*principem*	(acc. sing.)
	nitente:	*serua*	(abl. sing.)
	commorantum:	*mulierum*	(gen. pl.)
	conflagrantibus:	*moenibus, ceteris*	(dat./abl. pl.)
	circumiens:	*Cicero, mulier*	(nom. sing.)

3 (a) Verres was standing on the shore, leaning on a woman.

(b) (*Literally*) The pirate replied to them asking that he had seen the ships fleeing.

(*English*) When they asked him, the pirate replied that he had seen the ships fleeing.

(c) (*Literally*) The sailors being in need of food...

(*English*) Although the sailors were in need of food, Cleomenes did nothing.

(d) While Verres was making love to a woman, it was announced that the ship had been captured.

(e) You can see the ship ablaze with fire.

(f) They caught sight of the rest following a little more slowly.

(g) While waiting in Syracuse, the pirates saw the walls of the city.

(h) Verres said that he had not seen the ships approaching the harbour.
(i) No day is long for a busy man.
(j) Nothing is difficult for someone in love.

4 *Verre absente*
nautis sequentibus
populo inspiciente
nauibus ardentibus
Cleomene commorante
multitudine principem hortante

pp.265–6 Exercises

1 *eguissem etc.*
conflagrauissem
commoratus essem
secutus essem
acceptus essem
incensus essem
nisus/nixus essem
occidissem
sensissem
liberatus essem
accessissem

2 (a) When Cleomenes had fled, the others followed.
(b) Since the pirates had advanced very quickly, the last ships of the Romans were the first in danger.
(c) Although the commander had reached the shore quickly, the rest however were sailing more slowly.
(d) When Cleomenes had reached the shore with his ship, he hid (himself) at home.
(e) The rest also abandoned their ships since they had not been able to escape from the pirates by sea in any way.
(f) The leader of the pirates ordered the ships to be burned* when they had been captured.
* *incendi* = present infinitive passive – see *GVE* p.246.

3 (a) *cum imperator ad litus nauigauisset.*
(b) *cum naues incensae essent.*
(c) *cum praedones Syracusis commorati essent.*
(d) *cum moenia inspecta essent.*
(e) *cum multitudo incendium conspicata esset.*
(f) *cum nautae cibo eguissent.*

4

eguit	indicative perfect
conflagrasset	subjunctive pluperfect
tulerat	indicative pluperfect
recordatus esses	subjunctive pluperfect
constituisse	infinitive perfect
excogitaueras	indicative pluperfect
accepissent	subjunctive pluperfect
captus esse	infinitive perfect
occisi essent	subjunctive pluperfect
conspicati sunt	indicative perfect

p.267 Reading exercise/Test exercise

Thus the first ship to be captured was one belonging to the people of Haluntium. (*Literally*, a ship of the Haluntines was captured first.) In command of it was a nobleman from Haluntium, Phylarchus, whom the people of Locri afterwards ransomed from those pirates at public expense. Next a ship from Apollonia was captured and its captain Anthropinus killed. While these events were taking place, Cleomenes meanwhile had already reached the shore of Helorus. He had already rushed out of the ship on to land and had left his quadrireme bobbing on the sea. When their commander had disembarked onto dry land, the rest of the ships' captains followed Cleomenes closely.

p.267 English–Latin

1 (a) *multitudo naues ardentes conspicata est.*
(b) *reliqui praefecti nauium Cleomenem, cum in terram exiisset, secuti sunt.*
(c) *Cleomenes, cuius uxor in litore cum Verre erat, nauibus sequentibus e portu egressus est.*
(d) *praefecti nauium, cum mari praedones effugere non potuissent, principem secuti e nauibus egressi sunt.*

2 *praedones nauibus incensis Syracusas accedere constituerunt. audiuerant enim portum Syracusanorum pulcherrimum esse et sciebant se numquam nisi Verre praetore eum uisuros esse. quod cum statuissent Syracusas nauigauerant. piratica nauis Verre praetore, nostris nauibus ardentibus, usque ad portum Syracusanorum accessit. pro di immortales! o factum turpissimum!*

Section 4F

p.279 Exercises

1

Verb	Pres. subj.	Impf. subj.
concido	*concidam*	*conciderem*
hortor	*horter*	*hortarer*
morior	*moriar*	*morerer*
sum	*sim*	*essem*
timeo	*timeam*	*timerem*
aufero	*auferam*	*auferrem*
passive	*auferar*	*auferrer*
reuoco	*reuocem*	*reuocarem*
passive	*reuocer*	*reuocarer*
nauigo	*nauigem*	*nauigarem*

2

clamet	pres. subj.
amat	pres. indic.
dormiret	impf. subj.
auferret	impf. subj.
conspicatus esse	perf. infin. (deponent)
conati essent	pluperf. subj. (dep.)
dat	pres. indic.
dicetur	fut. indic. (passive)
excogitat	pres. indic.
curet	pres. subj.
nescirem	impf. subj.
cupiuisse	perf. infin.
loquitur	pres. indic. (dep.)
abstulisset	pluperf. subj.
monearis	pres. subj. (pass.)
accidat	pres. subj.
aget	fut. indic.
persuadet	pres. indic.
perficias	pres. subj.

3 **Indicative**

Verb	**Present**	**Imperfect**	**Pluperfect**
ago	*agit*	*agebat*	*egerat*
passive	*agitur*	*agebatur*	*actus erat*
perficio	*perficit*	*perficiebat*	*perfecerat*
commoror	*commoratur*	*commorabatur*	*commoratus erat*
libero	*liberat*	*liberabat*	*liberauerat*
passive	*liberatur*	*liberabatur*	*liberatus erat*
iaceo	*iacet*	*iacebat*	*iacuerat*
sequor	*sequitur*	*sequebatur*	*secutus erat*
nolo	*non uult*	*nolebat*	*noluerat*
accidit	*accidit*	*accidebat*	*acciderat*

Subjunctive

Verb	**Present**	**Imperfect**	**Pluperfect**
ago	*agat*	*agere*	*egisset*
passive	*agatur*	*ageretur*	*actus essat*
perficio	*perficiat*	*perficeret*	*perfecisset*
commoror	*commoretur*	*commoraretur*	*commoratus esset*
libero	*liberet*	*liberaret*	*liberauisset*
passive	*liberetur*	*liberaretur*	*liberatus esset*
iaceo	*iaceat*	*iaceret*	*iacuisset*
sequor	*sequatur*	*sequeretur*	*secutus esset*
nolo	*nolit*	*nollet*	*noluisset*
accidit	*accidat*	*accideret*	*accidisset*

p.281 Exercises

1 (a) Verres persuaded Servilius that he should go to Lilybaeum (to go to Lilybaeum).

(b) When he came to Lilybaeum, Servilius was flogged by the lictors.

(c) Verres had ordered the lictors to flog the man.

(d) Servilius, as a Roman citizen, begs Verres not to flog him nor to kill him.

(e) Just as Verres flogs Roman citizens, so I assert that he will himself be flogged by Roman citizens.

(f) Verres urges certain slaves not to spare Servilius nor to give help to him begging (when he begs for it).

2 (a) *ut Lilybaeum adeat*
(b) *ne abeatis*
(c) *ut Seruilium caederent*
(d) *ne taceret*
(e) *ut mihi credas*
(f) *ne quis fugiat neue abeatis*

p.282 Exercises

1 (a) It happens that Servilius speaks slightly too freely about the wickedness of Verres.
(b) Verres brought it about that Servilius came to Lilybaeum.
(c) It happened that Servilius, when he had come to Lilybaeum, was flogged by the lictors.
(d) Gavius, when he was in chains at Syracuse, said that he would bring it about that he would escape and come to Messana.
(e) Verres will bring it about that Roman citizens are killed.

2		***perficiam ut:***	**I shall bring it about that** (or **I shall manage to do):**
	(a)	*Verres Lilybaeum adeat.*	Verres comes to Lilybaeum.
	(b)	*uir a lictoribus caedatur.*	The man is flogged by the lictors.
	(c)	*serui eum ad terram adiciant.*	The slaves throw him to the ground.
	(d)	*uerberibus moriatur.*	He dies from the blows.
	(e)	*socii Romam profugiant.*	The friends escape to Rome.
		accidit ut:	**It happened that:**
	(a)	*Verres Lilybaeum adiret.*	Verres came to Lilybaeum.
	(b)	*uir a lictoribus caederetur.*	The man was flogged by the lictors.
	(c)	*serui eum ad terram adicerent.*	The slaves threw him to the ground.
	(d)	*uerberibus moreretur.*	He died from the blows.
	(e)	*socii Romam profugerent.*	The friends escaped to Rome.

pp.283–4 Reading exercise/Test exercise

This Gavius from Consa, of whom I speak, when he had been thrown into chains by this man among that number of Roman citizens and had escaped secretly by some method from the mines and had come to Messana, since he saw Italy and the walls of the people of Rhegium, Roman citizens, so near now, and since he had come back to life as if renewed from that fear of death and darkness by the light of liberty and some scent of the laws, began to speak at Messana and to complain that he, a Roman citizen, had been thrown into chains, that his route was directly to Rome and that he would face Verres as he arrived.

p.284 English–Latin

Verres uirum, cui Gauio erat nomen, in uincla coniecerat. qui perfecerat ut profugeret Messanamque perueniret. affirmauit se Verrem Romae delaturum esse. Verres autem, cum hoc audiuisset, seruis suis imperauit ut uirum caperent. illi in nauem ingredientem retraxerunt et ad magistratum duxerunt. Verres cum Messanam peruenisset, imperauit ut Gauius medio in foro nudaretur et caederetur. lictores ei oranti clamitantique se esse ciuem Romanum non pepercerunt. itaque accidit ut ciuis Romanus a Verre necaretur.

Section 4G

p.292–3 Exercises

1 (a) If Verres' father were here, he would judge his son to be an enemy of our state.

(If Verres' father had been here, he would have judged his son to be an enemy of our state.)

(b) If we were to pardon Verres, we should be stupid.

(c) If Verres were to demand my cups, I should send a letter to him without delay.

(d) Even animals if they heard these things would be moved.

(Even animals if they had heard these things would have been moved.)

(e) Unless you kept on shouting that you are a Roman citizen, you would be killed.

(f) If you had this protection, even the enemy would spare you.

(If you had had this protection, even the enemy would have spared you.)

(g) If there were foresight, there would be no evil.

(h) Wine prepares the mind (gets you in the mood) for lovemaking, unless you should have too much.

2 (a) *si ciuis Romanus essem ...*

(b) *si praesidium postulet ...*

(c) *si mora non esset ...*

(d) *si amici commoueantur ...*

(e) *si praesidium postularemus ...*

(f) *si clamitem ...*

(g) *uelim dicere ...*

(h) *uellem rogare ...*

(i) *postularem ...*

(j) *commouear ...*

p.297 English–Latin

Quamquam Gauius Raecium cognitorem nominauerat (cum ... nominauisset), litteras ei non misisti. uelim, Verres, te hoc mihi dicere. cur moratus es? cur statim litteras non misisti? nonne Gauius 'si litteras ad Raecium mittas' inquit 'me ciuem Romanum esse dicat. si adesset, me quem accuses innocentem esse affirmaret.' sed tu, Verres, summa Gauii neglegentia crucem parauisti. si bestiis hanc rem narrarem hae etiam commouerentur.